KEEPING WATCH OVER

SOULS

THE 6 MARKS OF A CHURCH THAT MAKES DISCIPLES

Mike Falkenstine

Table of Contents

Acknowledgments

With a book project like this one, I have a lot of people to thank and acknowledge because it really does take the contributions of a number of people to complete a book like this. Although I'm sure I'll forget people I should be acknowledging, allow me to thank and acknowledge some of the key people who come to mind:

As I mention in the book, I've always had a loving, respectful but 'I wonder why more is not happening here' relationship with the church. I am thankful to God that He didn't allow me to give up on His church, the Bride of Christ. May God use this book to strengthen churches around the world for His Glory!

I want to thank my wife Sherie for her continual support of my work toward creating resources and training that leads people to find Great Commission fulfillment.

To my three kids, Sarah Elizabeth, Isaac and Anna: You all are great people and I'm thankful that God allowed me to be your dad. Love you all!

If God chooses to bless your life as He has blessed mine, you'll to meet someone like my dear friend W. Brad Miller. When Brad and I met in 1991, I was on a path toward ambivalence toward God and the Bible. My parents had recently divorced, I was confused about my place in the world and I was not in a good place. Brad began meeting with me and God used our times together to change the course of my life. Anyone who does not believe in the power of one-on-one discipleship is wrong—I am living proof. Brad, it is your investment in me that has led to this book, the hundreds of thousands of people in China and around the world that have been impacted through what God has done in my ministry. I praise God for you!

How wonderful to get into a rhythm with a book editor, and I think that is happening with myself and Polly Lott. Polly, may I once again to thank you for your diligent, excellent work and I look forward to working together on future book projects! And thank you Tricia Heyer for introducing us to each other.

Finally, I am thankful for the Staff at Watermark Community Church in Dallas. This church is an example of how a church really can take the Bible and use it as a complete guide for biblical church. In particular, let me thank Jeff Ward, Haley Stringer, Jon Elmore, John McGee, Stacy Kirby, Natalie Morrison, Todd Wagner, Rick Wisner and Kate Romero. You all are so overabundantly generous with your time and knowledge... Thank you all!

Introduction

The 1956 Rose Bowl, which pitted the Michigan State Spartans against the UCLA Bruins, was an interesting game for Dave Kajzerkowski. As a sophomore tight end for the Michigan State Spartans, he had transferred from Notre Dame where he had played the 1955 campaign. After four years of reporting as an outstanding athlete and four-year football letterman for the Alpena, Michigan High School Wildcats, the sportswriters in Kajerkowski's hometown had tired of spelling out "Kajzerkowski" in their stories and had shortened the name to "Kaiser." At Alpena High, Kaiser had been an outstanding running back, but by the time he had transferred from Notre Dame to Michigan State, he had asked to switch from playing running back to tight end. Kaiser had also been recruited to be one of three kickers on the team, mainly handling longer field goal tries; however, an early season leg injury in the game against Michigan knocked Kaiser out of his kicking duties for most of the season. When out of uniform, Kaiser, who wore thick, plastic-rim glasses, looked more like a graduate assistant than a football player. He sometimes wore contact lenses, but he had accidently left them behind in his hotel room as the team left for the Rose Bowl game on the team bus. The 1956 Rose Bowl was a close affair. In the fourth and final quarter, the game was tied 14-14 with just seconds to play. After a pass completion put the football on the 24-yard line, the Michigan State head coach instructed Kaiser to kick the winning field goal with two seconds left. It was to be only his third field goal try of his college career! Gerald Planutis, the first-string field goal kicker, had missed a field goal earlier in the fourth quarter, so the coach gave Kaiser a chance to win the Rose Bowl for Michigan. There was one problem, however: Kaiser had neither his contact lenses nor his glasses with him at the Rose Bowl game. Kaiser figured that if he could see the ball once it was snapped, he'd be all right. As Kaiser was in the middle of a practice kick, the center, (the lineman who snaps the ball off the line of scrimmage) apparently confused, snapped the ball to the holder early and Kaiser was forced to give it a half-kick--but made fairly solid contact with the ball. The football began to veer to the left through the air as it left Kaiser's line of vision. Without his contact lenses or glasses, he couldn't see if it was on its way between the goalposts or if it would veer too far left. As all the other players and those in the stands watched the flight of the ball, Kaiser is seen looking directly at the referee who was standing behind him. Only when the referee held up his arms to indicate that the field goal was good did Kaiser know that he had made the kick successfully! As an interesting side note, the Planutis-Kaiser substitution was such a surprise, that announcers and reporters initially credited the game-winning field goal to Planutis! Kaiser's father, who was in the stands for the game, did not know his son was the player who had kicked the winning field goal until after the game, when his son told his dad that he was the one who kicked it through the uprights! As I look at the Western church landscape, many church leaders seem to be like Dave 'Kaiser' Kajzerkowski in the 1956 Rose Bowl. We're in the field of play, we want to do our best, but we're 'flying blind,' unable to see the goal that we want to hit and unsure if we're getting the 'ball down the field' far enough. I don't need to visit your church personally to know that you got into church ministry because you have a deep heart for Jesus, for people and for the good of the universal church. I'm writing this book as a guide for church pastors and leaders to be reminded of the greatness of our God, His incredible love for us and for the local church specifically, and His intention to do something great for His name today, in the world and in your local community. And if you're willing, He would love to use you and your church!

Becoming a disciple making church, while an incredible challenge for many churches, is worth your time and effort. Realize now that disciple making, what many church leaders call discipleship, is not just a program you install twice a year, but rather an all-encompassing culture shift in everything your church does. I hope and pray that this book is a small cog in the puzzle of what God wants to do in and through your church. In this Introduction, I'd like to look briefly at two areas: (1) Let's define the biblical purpose of the church, thereby setting the course for the rest of the book, and secondly, allow me to set the stage for why being a disciple-making church is so critically important in our world today. What is the biblical purpose of the local church? As we look at the biblical purpose of the church, I'd like to begin by identifying and diagnosing two common but unbiblical views of the primary purpose of the church. By describing these unbiblical views, we'll be able to understand more clearly what the Bible says about what a church should be.

In the first view, the local church exists for reaching the lost. Often these churches identify as 'seeker sensitive.' In this approach, the primary purpose of the local church is to draw in the unbeliever to the Christian faith. Since reaching the lost is the over-reaching goal of this church, everything that happens should be done according to the perceived needs of the non-believers, from the layout of the church building to the Sunday morning worship and teaching, in order to get as many unsaved people through the doors as possible. Theatrics and exciting musical entertainment, paired with state-of-the-art technology in lighting and sound are common in churches with this emphasis. The philosophy within this movement is that many people in our society are seeking God and want to know Him; however the idea of a "traditional" church scares them away from seeking Christ.

Scripturally, I view the Bible teaching just the opposite concept. The apostle Paul tells us that 'no one understands; no one seeks for God. All have turned aside…'[1] Until God Himself draws a person to Himself[2] and the Spirit awakens the heart, an unsaved person cannot believe. I would disagree with the concept that the unsaved know what they need most and that their spiritual desires would lead them to truth and salvation. As a result of this approach, the church ends up looking like the world because it has adapted to the world.

---

1. Romans 3:11-12
2. John 6:44

The second view we often see is that the local church exists for the needs of Christians. I have known many church leaders who push back on the 'seeker sensitive' model and say, 'The church exists for us! It exists to strengthen and serve Christians!' Instead of putting all its energy into evangelism, this type of church makes decisions based on the preferences of believers. While this view is closer to the priorities of the Bible, I think we are still missing the mark with this approach. By overemphasizing the needs and desires of Christians, the church can tend to neglect the Great Commission and the need for daily outreach to unbelievers. I've seen far too many churches become a Christian 'social club' where the needs and desires of the Christians outweigh everything else.

Todd Wagner, in his excellent book <u>Come and See: Everything You Ever Wanted in the One Place You Would Never Look</u>, uses an excellent illustration to illustrate this concern. He states that many people select churches much like they would a cruise ship. 'Whether consciously or otherwise, they ask certain questions that reveal their expectations. *Do I like the music in the ballroom? Do I like the captain and his staff? Do I get good service? Is it pleasant and comfortable? Do I like the experience enough to sail with them again?*[3] If the primary purpose of the church is to please Christians, it allows them to choose the features that are most pleasing to them, and to float through their church experience being mostly satisfied with the amenities of a particular church. It may sap their zeal for reaching the lost and being involved in God's Great Commission.

J.D. Greear says it this way: "Without the mission, a church is not a church. It's just a group of disobedient Christians hanging out."[4]

As we attempt to discover what the Bible says about the primary purpose of the local Church, we find no lack of source material there. My first 'go-to' passage of Scripture is always Acts 2! I love the early chapters of Acts because Luke wrote them on the heels of all the events we read about in the Gospels. Acts 1 records Jesus' ascension, and I can only imagine what the disciples were thinking and feeling! After all they had experienced and

---

3. Wagner, Todd. Come and See: Everything You Ever Wanted in the One Place You Would Never Look. Colorado Springs, David C Cook, 2017. p. 79
4. Greear, J.D. Gaining by Losing: Why the Future Belongs to Churches that Send. Grand Rapids, Zondervan

everything they had done with Jesus, their emotions must have been very raw—and now their question must have been 'What now?' I am thankful that the Apostle Luke records, in the Acts of the Apostles, the answer to that question.

In the first couple of chapters in Acts, some significant events were happening. The apostles began to organize themselves by choosing Matthias to replace Judas. Then the Holy Spirit came, as promised in Acts 1:8 and later in Acts 2, and there we read one of my favorite sermons by Peter. His words clearly cut to their hearts, and those who were present asked, 'Okay Peter, what now?'

His reply? "Repent and be baptized every one of you in the name of Jesus Christ for the forgiveness of your sins, and you will receive the gift of the Holy Spirit. For the promise is for you and for your children and for all who are far off, everyone whom the Lord our God calls to himself."[5]

Their response? Those who heard his reply were baptized, and 'there were added that day three thousand souls.'[6] We now have a church, three thousand strong on our hands! We see in the next verse then, what they were purposed to do: 'And they devoted themselves to the apostles' teaching and the fellowship, to the breaking of bread and the prayers. And awe came upon every soul, and many wonders and signs were being done through the apostles.'[7]

We see then in the very first local church ever to exist, the believers are receiving solid teaching, they are investing time together in fellowship, they are eating together, and they are praying together. As we read through the rest of the New Testament, the next big advancement in the progression of the local church comes as God calls a man that at one time was a major persecutor of Christians, Saul of Tarsus, to become the greatest church planter of all time! As the apostle Paul is planting churches, he has two things in mind: First, he is making and strengthening the disciples. Paul was not interested in "somewhat involved" believers. In Acts 14, he is doing ministry in Derbe with Barnabas, as we see that as 'they had preached the gospel to that city and had **made many disciples**, they returned to Lystra and to Iconium and to Antioch, **strengthening the souls of the disciples**, encouraging them to

5. Acts 2:38-39
6. Acts 2:41
7. Acts 2:42-43

continue in the faith, and saying that through many tribulations we must enter the kingdom of God.'[8] They were making fully devoted followers of Jesus, then strengthening them in the faith!

The second activity that we see Paul doing as he is planting churches is ensuring that each church had dedicated and trained elders. In the next verse in Acts 14, we read, 'And when they had appointed elders for them in every church, with prayer and fasting they committed them to the Lord in whom they had believed.'[9] Paul also gives us an additional hint into the purpose of the church as he is writing to the church at Ephesus, that, as the body of Christ, we are to be 'speaking the truth in love, we are to grow up in every way into him who is the head, into Christ.'[10]As the apostle Peter writes his first letter to a handful of churches in modern-day Turkey, he instructs them to: 'Keep your conduct among the Gentiles honorable, so that when they speak against you as evildoers, they may see your good deeds and glorify God on the day of visitation.' As we examine the New Testament, we begin to get a full picture of the purpose of the local Church. Taking these nuggets, together with the passages of the Great Commission that commands all Christians to preach the Gospel[11], make disciples[12] and be His witnesses[13],I've developed this biblical definition of the church:

> The biblical purpose of the local church is to glorify God[14] by worshipping Him, by edifying his people,[15] by proclaiming the Gospel of Jesus to the whole world,[16] and making disciples through the baptizing and teaching of new believers.[17]

Becoming a Disciple-Making Church Requires Focus

As we all know, if we want something done with excellence, it will require discipline, training and willpower. As an avid exercise fan, I love reading about the United States Navy Seal Team and the rigorous training it takes to be a Navy SEAL. The Navy SEALs (an acronym for SEa, Air and Land) are the most elite special forces in the United States. To become a Navy SEAL, one must go through some of the most demanding and arduous training of any military force in the world. Here's a quick look at a little of what it takes to be a Navy Seal:

8. Acts 14:21-22
9. Acts 14:23
10. Ephesians 4:15
11. Mark 16:15
12. Matthew 28:18-20
13. Acts 1:8
14. 1 Peter 2:12
15. Ephesians 4:15-16
16. Acts 1:8
17. Matthew 28:18-20

As one expresses an interest in becoming a Navy SEAL, an early step is to demonstrate the ability to complete preliminary medical and physical tests.

- In the first level of physical tests, standard minimum scores include completing a 500-yard swim in nine minutes or less, 90 or more push-ups and sit-ups in two minutes each, eighteen pull-ups, and a 1.5 mile run in combat boots in nine and a half minutes or less (extremely challenging to do without the combat boots!). These tasks must be done consecutively, with minimal rest time in between.

- If the candidate completes the first level of physical tests, a second level of physical tests must also be completed. To move on from the preparatory stage, individuals must swim 1000 meters with fins in 20 minutes or less and run four miles in boots and pants in 31 minutes or less, along with tests involving push-ups, sit-ups, and pull-ups.

- Those who fail are eliminated from the SEAL program and reclassified to other Navy positions. Of the people that start these preparatory phases, only 12% of all potential Navy SEALs make it to the next level!

Twenty-four weeks of Basic Underwater Demolition/Seal School comes next (also called BUD/S). Over the course of these six months, they conduct their 'Hell Week,' lasting for five days with only four hours of sleep each night. Common Hell Week training includes standing in waist-high cold water over long periods of time. The men are also required to carry Rubber Boats, most of the time above their heads, going through high waves and seas swells. Much has been made of the 200-pound logs carried by men in seven-member teams. The shivering-cold and salt-soaked trainees pick up a 150-pound log, run it over a fifteen-foot-high sand berm, drop it onto the sand, immediately pick it up again and press it over their heads, run the log into the ocean, and then carry the soaked, slippery log back through the soft sand *only to start all over again.* Additionally, Navy SEAL training includes close quarter combat training, parachuting and jumping into the ocean training. Trainees aren't just training their bodies, however, as they're also required to learn about tactics, strategy, and other subjects while pushing themselves to their physical limits. Only by completing BUD/S does a prospective SEAL even get the chance to enter SEAL Qualification Training, or SQT. At the end of their BUD/S training, only 1% of those who start, actually complete the training.

What is the point of all this training? The U.S. Navy is seeking to find the best of the best! When there is a covert or overt operation that no other soldier can do, the Navy SEALs are one of only two or three choices the U.S. Military consider. By successfully completing their rigorous training, they demonstrate themselves to be the elite of the elite—and they begin and complete missions that no one else can do. As examples, a Navy SEAL team captured Osama Bin Laden in Abbottabad, Pakistan, and another Navy SEAL team rescued Richard Phillips after his kidnapping off the ship Maersk Alabama by shooting his captors from 100 yards away while on a moving Navy ship!

As church leaders, each of us carry a tremendous burden and opportunity. As we'll look at in Chapter 1, church elders in particular carry a tremendous responsibility as laid out in Scripture. If the Navy is training their SEALs teams with this level of rigor to protect the United States, certainly we in church leadership must do our very best to "fight the good fight of the faith. Take hold of the eternal life to which you were called and about which you made the good confession in the presence of many witnesses."[18] God is calling all Christians to "always be prepared to make a defense to anyone who asks you for a reason for the hope that is in you"[19] and to "do your best to present yourself to God as one approved, a worker who has no need to be ashamed, rightly handling the word of truth."[20] How are you doing at making sure that all of the people in your church are able to make a defense of their faith and handle God's Word without shame?

As a church leader, creating a culture in your church that fosters true disciple-making will require incredible focus. As you build this focus, I offer this word of wisdom as one who has worked hard to become a disciple maker. Just like the men who don't make the cut with the Navy SEALS, you'll find that some individuals in your church will be 'all over the place' in terms of how well they track with you on this goal. As a friend pointed out to me recently, the Navy men who don't become SEALS are still good men and good soldiers! It is possible for these men to try three or four times to complete the rigorous training and requirements.

---

18. 1 Timothy 6:12
19. 1 Peter 3:15
20. Timothy 2:15

I started my ministry career on staff with The Navigators, an international, interdenominational Christian ministry that focuses on disciple making, I learned an old Navigator phase regarding discipling others: "many aspire, but few attain." This is hard work! Yet my encouragement to you as you read through these pages, and as you develop a new vision for your congregation of becoming skilled at being and making disciples, your focus should be upon getting each of your people to the same goal: to be a fully devoted follower of Jesus.

Along the way, just as you think things are getting even harder, you'll find that cream truly does rise to the top and those who begin to get it will lead and encourage others who may take longer. For your church to reach those in your church's geographic area, I believe that the first step is making sure that all those in our congregations are disciples of Jesus. Because disciples—those who are fully-devoted followers of Jesus—are individuals who are sold-out for Jesus and are willing to be used in any ways God asks them to share Jesus with others. Yet here's a principle you need to know: to be a church that is really good at being and making disciples, your pastoral and elder teams must develop a clarion call—in everything the church does, every program and every study--that you exist to be and to make disciples.

If that Navy SEAL team focus seems hard, here's the "up" side: a church full of disciples of Jesus can change the whole dynamic of your church and its ability to follow a command of Jesus to be "the salt of the earth" and allow our "light to shine before others, so that they may see your good works and give glory to your Father who is in heaven."[21]

So, although I am not advocating for you to take your congregation through a similar process like that of the Navy's prospective SEAL candidates, I do think that becoming a disciple-making church does require a singular focus to do it well, and a certain discipline on the part of the church leader.

In the pages ahead, I hope to give you that singular focus and a plan for how it can be done, thereby changing the dynamics of your church and the larger community in which your church serves.

Special Word to Senior Pastors

Before we launch into the rest of this book, I'd like to have a little

---

21. Matthew 5:16

conversation with the lead and senior pastors reading this book about your work and participation as leaders in a local church. If you are a pastor in a local church, I assume you entered this role because you love doing it and you've felt God calling you into this ministry. I'm sure that as you began doing church ministry, you began to notice ways that God was using your specific skills and spiritual gifts to grow and strengthen the local church you serve. To me, there is no better 'high' than this! You probably continued on in your ministry as you found God using you, and you began to see fruit from the time you invested in people's lives in the local church.

But somewhere along the way, something happened. Perhaps it was the 5,468th time someone tried to tell you how to do your job, or that last complaint about your preaching or the color of the carpet in the sanctuary, or the lack of snacks in the lobby on Sunday mornings. Maybe it was the feeling that you and your small team do all the work in the church (since you are the "paid professionals") and you have felt burned out and marginalized. The weight of ministry can get so heavy! So, you slowly began to figure out the least you must do to keep your job, because at your age, it'd be hard to do something different and start over with a new career. Maybe your talent in public speaking has allowed you to keep your job, and this may seem to be the path of least resistance toward retirement.

If this describes how you have felt or are feeling right now, may I speak to you as "ministry leader to ministry leader?" Because, I get it.

In my own ministry, I experienced ministry burnout in 2013 as the stress and pressure to keep up with fund raising, ministry projects and family life bore down on me. Not until 2017 did I really begin to feel that I was making my way back to the emotions I had felt before. I know personally how the heavy load of ministry can bear down with a crushing weight. According to www.leadershipresources.org, 1,500 pastors leave the ministry *each month* due to moral failure, spiritual burnout, or contention in their churches. Eighty percent of pastors and 84% of their spouses feel unqualified and discouraged in their roles. Additionally, 50% are so discouraged that they readily admit their willingness to leave the ministry if they could but have no other plan for making a living.[22]

If any of these statistics describe your situation today, let me first tell you 'thank you for your service.' I often say that ministry is a long slog and this

---

22. https://www.leadershipresources.org/blog/christian-ministry-burnout-prevention-signs-statistics-recovery/

career is a lot harder than most people in your congregation will ever know! If you fall into any one of these statistics, may I seriously recommend that you get the help you need to get spiritually, emotionally and relationally healthy? There are a lot of online resources now[23] that can also be of help, and I know a number of Christian counselors who specialize in helping ministry leaders recover from burnout. Your church needs you to be well and to search for and find that 'first love' for God and His work in the local church.

I also encourage you to pray much about what God is doing through this season of burnout or discouragement. We know that there are no mistakes in His economy, and He wants to use this season in your life for His own purposes. If, during this time, you do not or cannot recover a deep love for ministry in the Church, potentially the greatest thing you could do is find out what other career might kindle a passion within you. The local church does not need 'phoning it in' pastors and ministry leaders! Mike Ditka, the Hall of Fame NFL player and coach says "In life, many men have talent. But talent in itself is no accomplishment. Excellence in football and excellence in life is bred when men recognize their opportunities and then pursue them with a passion."[24] You may have talents in public speaking or leadership, but to create a church that makes disciples requires pursuing ministry with a passion.

As you continue reading this book, may I offer some encouragement for you? Leading your church toward being excellent at being and making disciples is the best thing you can do for yourself and your well-being, because as you will see, it is a model that encourages and in fact, requires a continual 'giving-away' of the ministry—and as more disciples in your church step up to serve, there are less requirements on you.

Leading your church to become a disciple-making church may be the hardest thing you'll ever do, especially if many of these Marks are not common in your church. It's going to take everything you have, with a deep passion to lead your church in potentially new directions. Your heart must be completely into the task. God wants to use you in this way, if you are willing to pour your whole heart into becoming an expert at making disciples.

As you'll read in the pages that follow, you'll need to focus on more 'doing' in addition to 'talking.' Our churches must become disciple-making factories, because more people in your churches living as fully devoted

---

23. I personally found Carey Nieuwhof's blog content on burnout to be particularly helpful. https://careynieuwhof.com/?s=burnout
24. https://www.youtube.com/watch?v=pSqdRMi3TNw

followers means more people reaching non-believers for Christ! Whole communities begin to change as God uses these new disciples, which then leads to a movement of God in the area where you live. It is my privilege to lead you on this journey, and I am hopeful that God will use this title in a mighty way in your life and the life of your congregation!

1

Keeping Watch Over Souls

Having daily routines is good for us. Current research has shown that having a daily routine can improve our overall health, well-being and productivity. Over the course of our adult lives, many of us try to tweak our daily routines to make ourselves more productive and waste less time.

In addition to daily time in God's Word, one of the consistent parts of my morning routine is to try and get at least thirty minutes of exercise at least five days a week. I love running and have been a runner since middle school, but as I approached my late 40's, my knees began to revolt at the idea of running five days a week! To help my knees, I now cycle three days a week and run only two days a week. As I'm cooling down from my exercising, I sit on my back patio and move on to another part of my morning routine. I love reading the morning newspaper, and because I live in Denver metro area, I read the digital replica edition of the Denver Post. I enjoy catching up on the news I may have missed over the last 24 hours, and even though all of the content that I read is readily available through other online sources, the Denver Post has taken the time to put the top news stories into one place for me—plus I get to read up on local news and sports teams (Go Broncos!).

While I love reading the whole paper every morning, one section that I enjoy the most is the advice column from the Chicago Tribune's Amy Dickinson called Ask Amy. While the column is nationally syndicated, I learned recently that the Denver Post is one of the few newspapers that carry her column in its full form and not in an abbreviated version, so I get to read the full column in my Denver Post. People seem surprised when I tell them that an advice column is be my favorite part of reading the morning newspaper! I usually explain that, of the three spiritual gifts I believe I have both through testing and experience, one of those is the spiritual gift we see in 1 Corinthians 12 and Hebrews 5 called discernment, or as it is sometimes known, discerning between spirits. The Greek word that we see in the Bible for discernment generally means being able to distinguish, discern, judge or appraise a person, statement, situation, or environment. So as I read the letters that come Amy in her column, I like to play a little game. After reading the letter and taking a minute to think about what type of advice the writer is asking of Amy, I like to come up with my own advice that I would give to the writer before I read the advice Amy has chosen to offer! I am happy to report that somewhere in the neighborhood of 75% of the time, Amy and I give essentially the same advice!

Our advice is very similar for several reasons, the biggest of which is that wonderful attribute we like to call 'common sense,' which the Merriam-Webster Dictionary defines as, 'sound and prudent judgment based on a simple perception of the situation or facts.'[1] It seems to me that this simple perception we call common sense seems to be missing at times as people write to Amy for advice! From the lady who was mad that a holiday dinner wasn't held up for them because they were 45 minutes late, even though she knew what time dinner was to start (and the food would all get cold!), to the daughter upset that her 75-year-old dad recently got a puppy, as she felt he was being inconsiderate to potentially leave a dog behind that would outlive him (though dogs are great for everyone, especially an older widowed man who just wanted some companionship!), much of the advice is made clear through common sense!

Of all the letters Amy publishes, the hardest to read about are from the young women who write in about a non-committal boyfriend. They generally go something like this:

> 'Dear Amy, my boyfriend and I have been dating for six years and while he says he loves me, he does not seem to want to get married. He will often tell me that he too wants to get married and two years ago, he asked me to move in with him, but I continue to wait on him

1. https://www.merriam-webster.com/dictionary/common%20sense

to take our relationship to that next step. I love him and want to marry him, but how much longer should I wait?'

I wanted to shout through my Samsung tablet to the young lady, "If after dating you for SIX YEARS he has not yet asked you to marry him and you really would like to be married, it's time for you to find a new guy! This one has had plenty of time to make preparations toward marriage! And as a side note, young lady, by moving in together, you are giving him many of the benefits of being married without him actually having to make the commitment!"

Over the past 25 years of my own full-time ministry, with much of that time making disciples and working to help local churches become disciple-making churches, many churches seem to resemble the boyfriend in this scenario. They want all the benefits of having people come to their church without making a full-commitment to helping those people to grow spiritually and become a disciple-making body of believers. There will be some who disagree with me, but look around at our churches today. I think if you took an honest assessment of the churches in our communities, many are not seeing a disciple-making movement spring up from their church body. Church mission statements run from the 'our mission is to learn more about Jesus, live more in Jesus, and love more like Jesus,' to the 'we exist to glorify God by making disciples,' to everything in-between. These mission statements are a good start, but I am most interested in the end result.

Here's my point: Writing a mission statement because your church thinks that it needs one is easy, but it's another thing to ensure that you are actually doing it well. (This 'what we say vs. what we do' will become a familiar theme throughout this book.) In this chapter, I want to address two main points: First, I want to give a challenge to your elders to become a disciple-making church, and secondly, I want to offer you a great 'first step' starting point. Since I defined the biblical purpose of the church in the Introduction, I am compelled now to take a look at those who are charged by God to oversee the local church: the elders of that church.

Throughout my Christian life, I've had an interesting history with the local church. Although I've always been open to serving on a church elder board, for a multitude of reasons, I've never been available when asked to become an elder of the churches where we've participated as members. Part of that is the nature of my ministry over the years, which has kept me out of the country and away from home for long periods, and another part is that we've not stayed at a church long enough for me to participate as an elder.[2]

Fortunately, as we seek to know the requirements of a church elder, the Bible provides clear requirements in 1 Timothy 3 and Titus 1 of how an elder of the church should live and lead. By my count, we see twenty-one combined requirements in both the 1 Timothy 3 and Titus 1 passages[3], accounting for requirements that are repeated in both passages. Look at this combined list:

- Above reproach
- The husband of one wife
- Sober-minded
- Respectable
- Not quarrelsome
- Manages his own household well, with all dignity keeping his children submissive
- His children are believers and not open to the charge of debauchery or insubordination
- He must be respected by outsiders, so that he may not fall into disgrace, into a snare of the devil.
- Not arrogant
- Not quick-tempered
- Not a drunkard
- Not violent
- Not a recent convert, or he may become puffed up with conceit and fall into the condemnation of the devil
- Not greedy for gain
- Hospitable
- A lover of good
- Self-controlled

2. This is primarily because our last two churches have had either a pastor fall into sin or get power-hungry, causing us to carefully examine our participation.
3. Combined list of the biblical requirements of an elder from 1 Timothy 3:1-7 and Titus 1:6-9

- Upright
- Holy
- Disciplined

Without breaking down the meaning of each of these requirements, a couple of notes about this list seem necessary for our understanding. First, only the exceptional man would meet all twenty-one of these requirements—a special individual whom God has been working in and through for some time, and one who has been open to God's work in his life. Secondly, I am struck by the fact that there is no indication biblically that it is acceptable to select men to be elders for your church who meet some of these qualifications. I've seen how easy it can be for church leaders to think, 'This guy meets 15 of the 21, and that's close enough! The qualifications he doesn't possess, another elder will have, and we don't want to be too judgmental since none of us is perfect.'

While you certainly want to select men who are stronger in certain areas than others, it seems clear that each elder needs to meet each of the 21 qualifications. As one of my proofreaders Lisa mentioned about this topic, 'I've seen far too often how unqualified elders never lead people to a greater degree of faith and obedience than they themselves possess. People who want to grow beyond the limitations of unqualified elders will leave your church.'

For those men who are nearly but not quite qualified, you then have a good opportunity to begin meeting with them for weekly Bible study and mentoring them toward qualification. You'll then have men 'in the hopper,' some of whom will become qualified as they grow in needed areas of their lives, and some who may never get there, but you'll still have had the opportunity to help them grow in their walk with Christ.

As you can see, elder selection is a hard process, but as you persist, you'll find men who meet all the qualifications, which will be of great benefit to your church.

As I look over these twenty-one qualifications, I think by God's grace that if one were to examine my life, I would generally meet those qualifications. Clearly, we're all sinners and saved by grace, and so I'm certainly not perfect—but I believe my life holds up to the standards for an elder that we see in these passages. If I were asked to be an elder, none of these requirements would wake me up with worry at 3am. I have, however, often told people that there are two additional requirements of an elder in the Bible that many people don't talk about, but that might wake me up at 3am with concern if I had the responsibility of an elder at a local church.

We find the first of these requirements in Acts 20 as the Apostle Paul the church planter gives instruction to the elders of the church at Ephesus during his journey through Asia. Of the many instructions he gives, Paul tells them to 'Pay careful attention to yourselves and to all the flock, in which the Holy Spirit has made you overseers, to care for the church of God, which he obtained with his own blood.'[4] There's a lot in this verse: First, pay attention to yourselves, meaning, watch your life and make sure you are meeting the 21 requirements of a biblical elder. Next, pay careful attention to all the flock, and by the way, this is the flock that the Holy Spirit gave you oversight of, and the flock that has been purchased by the very blood of Jesus! Yikes! That's enough to keep one up at 3am!

What is my point here? Being an elder is a BIG responsibility, and if I were to serve as an elder, I'd certainly want to do the absolute best job I could, not missing anything, seeing that this job was given to me by the Holy Spirit Himself. The flock He has asked me to oversee was bought with a high price!

The second of the "awake at 3am" verses is found in the book of Hebrews. As we near the end of Hebrews, we see what is often found at the end of the letters in the New Testament. The writer will often ask for prayer for some in his travelling group or will give final words of advice. In the last chapter of Hebrews, as the author is giving these same last words of encouragement, he writes, 'Obey your leaders and submit to them, for they are keeping watch over your souls, as those who will have to give an account. Let them do this with joy and not with groaning, for that would be of no advantage to you.'[5]

Although this passage is often used by elders to exhort their congregation that biblically they should obey them (and they should), I actually want to look beyond that initial instruction. If you look at this passage from the viewpoint of an elder, it brings a daunting responsibility of the church elder to light! Why should your congregation obey you as a church leader? Because you are keeping watch over the souls of the congregation. What does that even look like, to keep watch over people's souls? (Yes, it's 3am and I'm awake! I'm responsible for keeping watch over people's souls!) And

---

4. Acts 20:28
5. Hebrews 13:17

that's not all: As an elder who keeps watch over people's souls and as he does his earnest best to watch over the souls of those in the congregation in a way that honors Jesus, the elder will have to 'give an account.' The Greek word for 'give account' in this passage in Hebrews is Logos, which in English means 'a speech or discourse.' So, what do we learn about this expectation? As elders are keeping watch, they will have to give a speech on how well they did in that role, presumably after their earthly life is over.

If I were an elder of a local church, I'd want to make sure that I could give a good account in this heavenly speech I'm going to be required to give!

We then get to the heart of this book: given the biblical purpose of the local church and the immense responsibility that those who are called to oversee the church have, I want to help church leaders succeed in both of these areas. Although this is a book about the Six Marks of a Church that makes disciples, you'll also find this book will help you both in the area of fulfilling the biblical purpose of your church—and to help you sleep past 3am as you get a handle on how to 'keep watch' over your people and see them grow into fully devoted followers of Jesus! That's what we exist to do at One Eight Catalyst, the ministry I oversee; we exist to create resources and deliver training that is a catalyst enabling every Christian to find Great Commission fulfillment. The more people in your church become disciples of Jesus, the more they will find out how God has uniquely equipped them to find Great Commission fulfillment.

Great First Step: Clarifying the Mission of Your Church

Before I address the Six Marks of a Church that makes disciples, I firmly believe that the first task in developing a church that makes disciples is to have a God-given, clearly articulated and widely accepted mission statement. A church mission statement is simply a 'here's what we exist to do' statement that clearly lays out your church's purpose—why it exists. And before you say, 'Mike, we already have a mission statement,' I would ask you a few questions:

- Does it define what your church does?
- Does everyone on your church staff come to work knowing what this church exists to do, and do they often repeat it to others as they do their

work in church ministry?

- Finally, do all the people in your congregation know the mission statement, and as they volunteer their time and give of their financial resources, do they know they are doing both of these for the advancement of the mission statement, that is repeated often and known by all?

I would say that if the answer is 'No' to any of these questions, revisiting the mission statement is important! If there is not a God-given, clearly articulated and widely-accepted reason why your church exists, you can't lead people to a place that isn't widely identified and known. Certainly, as you'll see throughout the chapters of this book, to become a church that makes disciples requires intentionality and a clear path in which to lead your people.

The steps for the leadership team (and the elders specifically) to review your current mission statement (or in some cases, to create a mission statement for the first time) are relatively simple and straightforward. Sitting down first to talk with your staff and later, with the elders, to answer the question, 'Why does this church exist and what purpose does God want us to be running hard after?' can we a very rewarding and challenging task!

First, you want to ask what the Bible instructs you all as a church to be doing. What is the biblical role of the local church? If you recall from this book's Introduction, I have done my best to help answer that question. Here's my answer again for your use in this process:

> The biblical purpose of the local church is to glorify God[6] by worshipping Him, by edifying his people,[7] by proclaiming the Gospel of Jesus to the whole world,[8] and by making disciples through the baptizing and teaching of new believers.[9]

As you meet with your staff and the elders, you may come up with a slightly different answer, but remember the very common biblical interpretation principal that a doctrine (a teaching) cannot be considered "biblical" unless it sums up and includes all that the Bible says about it. So dig deep and find out what the biblical purpose of the church is. This can be a very rewarding process as each staff member brings his or her own study to the table, and together you find out all that the Bible says about the local church.

Secondly, once you feel you have a good handle on what the biblical

---

6. 1 Peter 2:12
7. Ephesians 4:15-16
8. Acts 1:8
9. Matthew 28:18-20

purpose of the local church is, answering the question of 'What is God putting on our hearts to do?' is a great next step. This would include looking back at the history of your church (if you are not a new church plant), and recalling why God called the founders of your church when it was first planted. While we want biblically-based mission statements, there is a little leeway in this process based on what God has done and what He is now doing. For example, if you look back at the history of your church and find that God continues to bring evangelists and people who have a heart for the lost, this knowledge would be something to keep in mind when revising or writing a new mission statement. What is unique about your church and what words describe your church? These are all factors to look at and talk about. In this process, as you are getting great feedback from staff, elders and potentially, key volunteers, a picture should begin to emerge based on what God has done, what it seems that He is currently doing, and where He wants your church to go in the future. It could be that going through this book will help you define what He is doing as well.

If you all determine that you are weak in a couple of these Marks and you determine you want to strengthen them, this could help define what your church now exists to do.

The third step includes getting broad acceptance from key volunteers, staff and the elders. As you whittle down the true purpose that God has for your local church, testing it on a broad group of key people is important. For it to become a value that the congregation will buy into and want to invest in, I think it's important to have broad buy-in. Test it out on a group of key volunteers and members. What do they think? Is it easy for them to understand? Does it leave any question in their minds as to the meaning? These and other similar questions are important to ask.

Finally, I offer you a couple of other notes as you walk through this process. First, I would highly recommend that you try to keep your mission statement 'short and sweet.' I recently helped a church go through this process using a 49-word mission statement! The end result of such a long mission statement was that because it was hard to remember, no one memorized it, it wasn't repeated often, and it ended up being put on a back page of the church website, out of sight and mind!

A good general rule is that a mission statement should be 25 words or less. Of course, if your mission statement ends up being 27 words, that's fine. The bigger point here is that as you focus in on a mission statement that is biblically-based and has gained wide acceptance, do your best wordsmithing to eliminate any and every unnecessary word. Going back through it multiple times to make it as clear and simple as you can is worth your time and effort. Long words such as "sanctification" and "justification" are important to know and understand, but there's probably a better place for them than your mission statement.

Then, once you've developed a statement that the leadership team really likes and has bought into, the lead pastor, the elders and other pastors and ministry leaders should start talking about the mission statement all the time to the church. This frequent discussion reinforces why the church exists and enables others to join you in the direction that God is leading you together. A dedicated effort at all levels is required to do this well, but I guarantee that it is worth it!

I wholeheartedly believe that the very first steps toward becoming a Church that makes disciples include knowing why God organized your local church into existence based principally on a biblical foundation, together with the responsibilities that God gives to elders to pay sharp attention to the flock He's given you, watching over their souls. In the coming chapters, we will walk through Six Marks I've found in my experience and research of churches that make disciples, which is what I hope will be an end product of this book.

Imagine your church full of fully-devoted followers of Jesus.... Your church and the larger community in which it serves will never be the same again!

Discussion Questions

1. What key thoughts does this chapter spur in you? Is your heart stirred in a particular area, and if so, why do you think so?

2. As you look at the elder responsibilities detailed in Acts 20:28 and Hebrews 13:17, what encourages you and what challenges you?

3. What do you think of your church's current mission statement? Do most people on staff and most key volunteers know it by heart? If not, why not?

4. As you walk through the principles found in this book on developing a mission statement for your church, what is going well? What are the hardest parts of that process? Finally, what steps are you all taking to 'power' through the hardest parts?

2

The First Mark of a Church that Makes Disciples

High View of Scripture

After twenty-five years of full-time ministry, I've pretty much seen it all. I've loved just about everything I've gotten the chance to do. There is one pet peeve I've developed however in an otherwise pet peeve-less existence. I've gone back and forth about this annoyance of mine, if I'm hitting the mark and should keep it up or if I should show more grace. When I send a ministry or personal email or text to someone, I generally expect a reply within 24 hours. I think that shows that the recipient is being thoughtful and respecting my time, and they rightly assume that I am waiting for the reply before I can continue with my work or project. Because I want to communicate to other email or text users that I respect them and their time, I have written into the staff policy manual of our Christian non-profit a requirement to reply within 24 hours.

Now, I know what some of you are thinking, 'Mike, take a chill pill. What if people are on vacation or just are hitting a busy spot in their schedule?' Yes, I know there are times when replying with my 24-hour window is not feasible, but during times of busyness, I think we all have a few seconds we can at least scratch out a 'Mike, so sorry, super busy, can I get back to you in a week?' Yay, I love that! The twenty seconds it took to send a quick response that means to me, 'Mike, super busy, but I love you brother and I'll get back to you as soon as I can.'

Yes, of course, please take your vacation! I don't expect much from you while you take time off with family. I have no problem with that at all. Interestingly, in doing some on-line reading, it seems like the interwebs back me up.

A recent study from researchers at the University of Southern California's Viterbi School of Engineering found that when coworkers or team members are working on a particular project together, more than 70% of people expected a response within four hours, while almost 30% expected a response within one hour. I'm happy to report that the study results showed that the most common email response time is two minutes. Half of responders in the study responded to the email in just under an hour. Reading this study makes me happy! It seems like the majority of professional people feel the same way that I do: it's good to reply to email quickly.

I wonder, then about the worst of the offenders, the ones who really put the pet in my peeve. I have known people well who have committed that they will reply within 24 hours, and sometimes even, as a show of 'I love all people' have added to their email signature a statement like, 'I commit to reply to your email promptly, at the latest 24 hours,' only to then not reply at all for no stated reason at all. There was no story later about a trip to the Emergency Room or no unforeseen trip back to their hometown. They just fell of the map and didn't reply. The first Mark of a Church that Makes Disciples is a church that believes the Bible is the inspired Word of God and communicates to the congregation its value and worth. This is a Church that has a high view of Scripture, and communicates to all in the church that we are a church that invests time in the Bible and we look to the Bible for our 'marching orders.' This type of church takes making disciples seriously! This concept may seem at first glance to be a given in the church community, but I am surprised by how many church leaders say with their mouth that the Bible is reliable and is the inspired Word of God, only to clearly not demonstrate that belief through their actions. Church leaders who say with their lips that the Bible is reliable in all areas of our lives but do not make that a priority in their ministry at their church is like the acquaintances and colleagues of mine who commit to replying to my email within 24 hours, but don't: their words and their actions don't match. In order to have a church that is a disciple-making church, the church leaders must determine both what the Bible is and then, if they agree that it is the inspired word of God, they must make extreme efforts to communicate that to their congregation. A good first step in this process is to re-examine the authority of God and the Bible.

The Authority of God and the Bible

The Merriam-Webster Dictionary defines authority as 'power to influence or command thought, opinion, or behavior.'[1] We may each have several people or entities that have some authority on or over our lives. But as we all know, God's authority on our world and on our lives has no limits. Within a biblical worldview, original authority and ultimate authority belong to God and God alone. No one gave it to Him, nor did He inherit it from anyone. God inherently embodies authority because He is 'I AM WHO I AM.'[2]

God is the creator of the heavens and the earth, He owns the earth and all that it contains and those who dwell in it.[3] In the end, God consumes it all as He declared, "Behold, I am making all things new."[4] To understand the fact of God's authority is as simple as accepting the fact of God Himself. The apostle Paul says it best in Romans 13 when he states, 'For there is no authority except from God, and those that exist have been instituted by God.'[5] Without question, God's authority reigns supreme in this world. The Bible talks about God's authority in much detail. We know that the Bible asserts that God is the true God[6], that His judgements are veracious and just[7], that a knowledge of God is a knowledge of the Truth[8]. We know that the Bible states that people who accept Christ are said to have found the truth[9] and the way of truth.

Here's the bottom line: this truth fleshes itself out in a logical argument as we apply deductive reasoning that the Bible is the Word of God and the words of God are authoritative because God is authoritative, so the conclusion we must draw is that the Bible is authoritative. John Frame, professor of Systematic Theology at Reformed Theological Seminary in Orlando crisply states, "There is no higher authority, no greater ground of certainty.... The truth of Scripture is a presupposition for God's people."[10]

1. https://www.merriam-webster.com/dictionary/authority
2. Exodus 3:14
3. Psalm 24:1
4. Revelation 21:5
5. Romans 13:1
6. John 3:33, 17:3, Rom 3:4, 1 Thessalonians 1:9
7. Rom 2:2, 3:7, Rev 16:7 and 15:3
8. Rom 1:18, 25
9. 1 John 2:27, 2 Thessalonians 2:13, Ephesians 5:9, and 1 John 3:19
10. John M. Frame, Apologetics to the Glory of God (Phillipsburg, NJ: Presbyterian and Reformed, 1994) 127.

This presupposition extends both to you and to those in your congregation. From your seat and as one guided by Acts 20:28 and Hebrews 13:17, allow me to offer a few practical suggestions on how you can drill home to your congregation this elevated view of the Bible as authoritative Scripture.

An Elevated View of the Bible

Preaching powerfully from God's Word

We all know the power of good preaching from God's Word. For the church leader who wants his congregation to know the power contained in God's Word, powerfully preaching and teaching from God's Word is a great first step.

Far too many pastors today seem to be overly worried about having a 'relevant' sermon for their people on Sunday morning. If we believe that the Bible has authority because God's authority is absolute, there should be nothing more relevant to our culture today than the Word of God.

The Bible transcends time, tradition and culture. To show your people of your church your high view of the power of the Bible, allow the text to do the talking, the preaching, the teaching and the transforming. We see throughout the New Testament that bold preaching ruled the day, both before the early church and during the days the first churches were being formed. John the Baptist came preaching in the wilderness, "Repent for the kingdom of God is at hand"[11] on the coming of the Lord Jesus. From the early days of the ministry of Jesus, he was stating "I must preach the good news of the kingdom of God," and He continued preaching the good news throughout the full course of His ministry. Throughout the book of Acts, we see the apostles 'every day, in the temple and from house to house, never ceasing to teach and preach that Christ is Jesus.'[12]

One of my heroes of the faith, the Apostle Paul preached the Gospel anywhere and at any time that he could. In his encouragement to the young church planter Timothy, he charged him 'in the presence of God and of Christ Jesus, who is to judge the living and the dead, and by his appearing and his kingdom: preach the word; be ready in season and out of season; reprove,

---

11. Matthew 3:2
12. Acts 5:42

rebuke, and exhort, with complete patience and teaching.'[13] Paul helps us bring the point home as he is writing back to the church at Rome. For Paul, as it should be for all those who are called as pastors and elders to preach and teach from God's Word, he states, 'For I will not venture to speak of anything except what Christ has accomplished through me to bring the Gentiles to obedience—by word and deed, by the power of signs and wonders, by the power of the Spirit of God—so that from Jerusalem and all the way around to Illyricum I have fulfilled the ministry of the gospel of Christ; and thus I make it my ambition to preach the gospel, not where Christ has already been named, lest I build on someone else's foundation'.[14] This is a man who wanted to make the name of Jesus known!

The message of Christ found in the Bible had become incarnational to Paul. He didn't want to preach anything outside of what Christ has already done in his own life. Paul had experienced the transformative power of Christ and His words, and the preaching came from a place of real-life experience. When you as a church leader preach and teach from the Bible from a place of 'I've experienced and seen the transformative power of the Bible myself and I want you to experience it too,' it brings the message of the Bible to a whole new level, and your people will follow you down those roads that you've already walked.

Setting the Expectation for Daily Time in the Bible

This is the second book in a series of books we use in our ministry at One Eight Catalyst. The first book is a book on the 6 Marks of a Disciple, in which I walk people through a workbook-style book that helps readers assess where they are in Christ and find the areas they can work on in their pursuit of becoming a fully-devoted follower of Jesus. I believe that a clear Mark of a Disciple of Jesus is that he or she is obedient to the Bible, knows God's Word, and seeks to obey the commands that are found in God's Word. All of this is pretty hard to do if the people in your congregation are not spending daily time in God's Word. Anyone who is doing well in their walk with Jesus is investing daily time in the Bible. As you already know, it's hard for God's Word to be "a lamp to our feet and a light to our path"[15] if it never

---

13. 2 Timothy 4:1-2
14. Romans 15:18-20
15. Psalms 119:105

gets picked up and read daily. As one who is 'keeping watch over their souls,'[16] think of ways to verbally encourage them and to even create a regular way of reminding them to be in God's Word daily.

Todd Wagner, Senior Pastor at Watermark Community Church is Dallas, TX, has developed a great way to encourage people toward daily reading. In talking to the staff at Watermark, I quickly learned during a recent visit that almost every time that they see Todd, the first thing that he asks them is 'So, what are you learning today from God's Word?' Interestingly, there are plenty of other topics that Todd wants to talk about, but the very first thing is this question about their time in God's Word. I love this for a couple of reasons: First, it indicates a lot about our priorities. 'Though there are many things we could talk about first, there is one thing I want to make sure we talk about.' This regularly-asked question shows that Todd, in his shepherding and oversight duties, knows that it's best for his people's spiritual growth to be in God's Word daily. This first question also demonstrates that, for the disciple who wants to know God and hear from God, communication happens primarily through the Bible. And what a way to re-set the culture at his church! This habit says, 'we are serious about making sure everyone is in God's Word daily.' It certainly sets a high standard.

I also like this because when congregation members and staff anticipate seeing Todd at church, they know the question is coming! 'I really want to have an answer when Pastor Todd asks me what I'm learning from my time in the Bible. I want to have an answer!' Developing a similar question or catch phrase is a great way to keep the Bible as a high priority.

I also believe that giving your congregation a number of tools to encourage Bible reading is a great idea. On your church website or app, providing a reading plan is a great way to show that reading the Bible is an expectation at your church. While there are a number of tools that could be employed, I highly encourage you to get creative in your efforts to get your people into God's Word! Create an environment that makes it clear that, at your church, daily Bible engagement is normal and expected and "what we do around here."

There is a valid reason for all of this Bible engagement. In his excellent book, *Move: What 1,000 Churches Reveal about Spiritual Growth*, Greg Hawkins undertook a six-year study to measure the spiritual growth of over

---

16. Hebrews 13:17

250,000 people in over a thousand churches of varying spiritual maturity. His findings were quite interesting:

> "We learned that the most effective strategy for moving people forward in their journey of faith is biblical engagement. Not just getting people into the Bible when they're in church - which we do quite well - but helping them engage the Bible on their own outside of church...... Nothing has a greater impact on spiritual growth than reflection on Scripture."[17]

In my own walk with Jesus, reflection on Scripture has had a significant impact, especially through the spiritual discipline of "scripture memory." Shifting the culture toward scripture memory as "It's just what we do around here" is another way to underscore that you as an elder or pastor don't just want your people to be hearing you preach; the practical application for each member of your congregation on their own is equally important.

In order to help the people in your congregation to continually move toward spiritual growth and, by extension, to become a fully devoted follower of Jesus, you must create an environment where it's completely normal for us to be talking about the Bible, encouraging one another from the Bible, asking one another what we're learning from the Bible, and even quizzing each other on Bible verses we've just memorized. These are all ways that you as a leader can create a 'Bible-first' culture.

If we believe, as the writer of Hebrews did, that 'the Word of God is living and active, sharper than any two-edged sword, piercing to the division of soul and of spirit, of joints and of marrow, and discerning the thoughts and intentions of the heart. And no creature is hidden from his sight, but all are naked and exposed to the eyes of him to whom we must give account',[18] then we want our people to be in God's Word *habitually*. We know of the sinfulness of man and how desperately we need to be pierced and have our thoughts and the intentions of our hearts examined. We know that God saves by the Bible, He sanctifies by the Bible, and He comforts, edifies and does all spiritual work by the Bible. The foundation of all Christian endeavor is the Word of God.

---

17. Hawkins, Greg L. Move: What 1,000 Churches Reveal About Spiritual Growth. Chicago: Zondervan, 2011.
18. Hebrews 4:12-13

Remembering that More is Caught than Taught

As you are probably well aware, your congregation watches you as a leader of your church. The ways that you obey the Bible and how you apply it to your own life will speak volumes to those who are watching how you handle God's Word. If you loosely obey Scripture in your own life, that speaks volumes to those in your congregation watching your life.

This can play itself out in a million different ways. For example, in your own life, have you developed a life plan and daily living plan that is based on God's Word? This may include everything from developing a plan on how you will choose to interact with those of the opposite sex to whom you are not married, to how you will make your personal financial decisions. Being able to quote Scripture and mention how those verses shaped your plan in these areas of your life speaks volumes.

The same is true for a entire elder board: To be able to say that a decision was made because of 'x,y,z Scripture verses,' and that careful prayer and study went into the decision as the elder board scoured the Bible for guidance, will be areas that you and the elder board can demonstrate to your congregation truly that 'All Scripture is breathed out by God and profitable for teaching, for reproof, for correction, and for training in righteousness, that the man of God may be complete, equipped for every good work.'[19] The process of being a disciple-making church includes deciding early on what you and your church believe about Biblical authority. This vital foundation defines the tenor of your ministry and will speak volumes to your congregation. Churches that do this well have an attitude that demonstrates, 'If the Bible says it, we do it!' Raising the value and transformative power of Scripture keeps your church firmly rooted in God's Word for all personal and ministry decisions, and will keep you from the temptation that many churches have fallen into: taking the Scripture we want to obey and disregarding the parts we don't like. According to passages like 2 Timothy 3:16, all of Scripture is authoritative or none of it is.

There is an old saying that "we can't 'pick and choose' which Bible verses we obey." Raising the authority of the Bible also separates your church from the temptation that can creep in and lead to a very watered-down

---

19. 2 Timothy 3:16-17

version of Christianity. Our Western Christian landscape is full of church denominations that have taken a 'preach through the papers, telling nice stories' kind of Christianity, which neuters the power that Christ alone has to transform lives! I have often referred to these churches as 'Christian social clubs' and not really churches at all. These are places where people go to meet friends, enjoy a nice potluck from time to time and hear a message on Sunday that makes them feel good and allows them to go on with the rest of their week without much interaction with God or His Bible, until next Sunday or the next watered-down event.

Theologian and author Carl F.H. Henry states this well. 'Without an authoritative Scripture, the church is powerless to overcome not only human unregeneracy (a state of persistent unrepentance) but also satanic deception. Where the church no longer lives by the Word of God, it is left to its own devices and soon is overtaken by the temptations of Satan and the misery of sin and death.'[20]

May I strongly encourage you to take the higher ground here and challenge both your congregation and church leadership to be in God's Word daily, emphasize the transformative power of Scripture. And as I close out this chapter, may I give you one more encouragement in this area? Pastors tell me regularly that they worry if they strike this tone with their church and and made it a 'requirement' to have this attitude toward Scripture, they may lose too many of their congregation because the 'requirement' will drive people away. In the vast research I've done for this book, plus the twenty-five years of experience in full-time ministry, I have seen a different story. Yes, you may lose some people, and also you'll be gaining people who want to get serious about their faith. As they engage daily in God's Word and see around them a church that has a very high view of Scripture, you'll gain so much more than you may lose.

In what will become a major theme throughout this book, people who attend your church want a high bar to reach for. When you challenge them to meet the high bar, more people will go for it than those who don't, and you want people at your church to be growing spiritually! People who are being transformed by God's Word and see their church leaders doing the same are more likely to share that transformation story with others, which leads

20. Henry, Carl F.H. "The Authority and Inspiration of the Bible," 13.

to numerous additional outreach and evangelism opportunities—and more stories of God at work in transforming the lives of your congregation.

Discussion Questions:

1. If you and your team were to do an honest assessment of what you are communicating—daily and weekly—to your congregation about the value of the Bible, what would that assessment be?

2. Are you and your team currently encouraging everyone at your church to invest time daily in God's word? If so, what does that look like? How could you do better in that area?

3. What tools does your church produce that communicate that everyone should be in God's Word daily? If you are not producing those tools, brainstorm together the ways you could be do that better - what does that list look like?

4. Do you worry that, if you talk a lot at your church about the transformative power of God's Word, it may result in people leaving your church? If so, talk and pray with your team about this, and determine together where this fear is really coming from.

3

The Second Mark of a Church that Makes Disciples

A Confident Expectation of Gospel Transformation

I find it easy to be amazed at all the technology that exists in my daily life. Consider my current "smartphone," for example: I really am amazed at all that it can do, especially when I think back to 1983 and how much phone technology has changed in that time! I was in 9th grade that year, and I needed to call my mom from a pay phone after basketball practice to come and pick me up. Occasionally, she would be out of the house either talking to neighbors or working in her garden, and she wouldn't hear the phone ringing—and that would create a problem for me! As I look back on those days, how I wish now that both of us could have had a mobile phone so that she could have heard the ringing right away!

Are you as amazed as I am at all the features we have with our Android or Apple phones today? Here's just a quick look at a few tasks that my phone can do for me: it can calculate current altitude, pay for my groceries, send mail-type communications instantly either through email, text or one of several messaging apps, and as I did just the other day, talk with no charges and from the comfort of my home in Colorado—with my daughter who is serving the Lord in China this summer. I can also read news, track workouts, review Scripture memory verses, and read one of over 1,900 Bible versions in over 1,300 languages on the Bible app! This list barely scratches the surface on the list of all the things this phone in my hand can do!! Wow! With the amazing variety of tasks that these phones can accomplish, it's easy to forget that they also can make wireless phone calls from wherever you happen to be!

For me, the most amazing feature on the phone is its ability to know where I am at all times and give me directions to where I need to go. Not that long ago, my wife and I used to annually buy the latest version of the *Rand McNally Road Atlas* for our travel for the year. I find it amazing that my phone is always communicating with multiple satellites 12,000 miles in space to calculate my exact location via the Global Positioning System (GPS) receiver embedded in my smartphone.

I'll never forget the first time the GPS got me out of a jam. I had gotten my first smartphone in 2008 and I was on vacation with my family in Florida. With the tall trees, we couldn't see any other buildings and we needed to purchase some items at Walmart. After typing in 'nearest Walmart,' it gave us precise directions to a Walmart that was only 1.5 miles away. Amazing! That was then I knew that phone technology had taken a big leap forward.

Although they have been around much longer than smartphones, the other technology I find amazing today is commercial airplanes. To be able to travel so far and at such a high rate of speed is incredible. Whenever I am on a flight, I marvel at all that is taking place. I am flying at over 500 miles an hour at over 30,000 feet above the earth, watching movies, eating food and able to talk with others on the flight! Isn't that so amazing? To think that I can leave my home airport in Denver and be in Beijing, China in 16 hours is truly incredible. Just a mere one hundred years ago, that trip required a 45-day (or more) voyage, first by train to San Francisco, then to China by ship (fraught with bandits on the railways and storms on the seas.) I am always perplexed when I hear fellow travelers complaining to airline employees, often about very petty or small things. I want to go over to these people and say, 'Do you not realize what we're actually getting to do here? We should be so thankful that we get to live in this era of time and get to participate in this process! It's *amazing!*' We can so easily lose perspective when something in our modern world doesn't work just the way we want it to—and then it's easy to complain. Whether our inconvenience is about our smartphone glitching or something not going smoothly for us at the airport, we complain and moan, forgetting the true power of technology to improve our lives! If we would simply remember what our lives were like *before* these technologies, we would gain perspective on whatever our complaint may be about.

The second Mark of a Church that Makes Disciples is the church's confident expectation that God will change people's lives. I am often surprised how many Western church denominations today do not have this expectation and are seemingly not calling all of their congregation to confidently expect major life change through their walk with Jesus. In our Western context, it's easy for us to grow complacent in our church life, forgetting whom we really serve and what our God is completely capable of doing! From the drug addict, to the guy addicted to porn, to the lady fighting an eating disorder, the God who is able to do 'abundantly more than all we could ever ask or imagine'[1] wants to set us free and give us a new life in Christ! The church that has this expectation can say, to whomever may walk through the doors of the church, the same words that Peter and John said to those who marveled at their healing of the lame beggar in Acts 3, "And his name—by faith in his name—has made this man strong whom you see and know, and the faith that is through Jesus has given the man this perfect health in the presence of you all."[2] Whether a person is physically lame, or has any number of other physical or emotional ailments, faith in Jesus restores it all!

A Reminder for Us All

This book, while available for all to read, is designed for church leaders in their varying capacities. Elders, pastors, and ministry staff are the people I have in mind as I write this book. You may be thinking, "Mike, we know about the transformative power of the Gospel. You don't have to walk us through this one." If that is what you are thinking, I am glad you have such confidence in the Gospel!

Here is where my motivation lies in this chapter: in my capacity with our Christian non-profit organization, I visit a lot of churches and I must say that the head knowledge many pastors and elders have about the transformative power of the Gospel is not matching the activity, the 'doing' in Church life today. Often in our churches, we confuse knowing about the

---

1. Ephesians 3:20
2. Acts 3:16

transformative power of the Gospel with doing, with calling each member to an expectation. James gives us a great baseline here as he writes, 'But be doers of the word, and not hearers only, deceiving yourselves.'[3] Church leaders and elders should be the first 'doers' and not just 'hearers,' especially in the area of letting people see what God is actively doing transformationally in their lives. A friend of mine told me recently that, in her experience, church leaders feel the temptation to conceal from their congregation their past weaknesses, how God has worked in and through them, because disclosing might undermine their authority in their churches. In my experience, just the opposite is true! When a leader says, 'I'm depraved in my flesh, and only because of what Christ has done in my life do I still live today, and please let me tell you about that story,' that the Gospel is communicated more powerfully and in a way that I can better relate to in my own life.

Knowing about something or even talking about something is not the same as doing it. Here's a quick example: would you get on an airplane if the person in the cockpit has been taught how to fly a plane and can talk to you about it, but has never actually done it? In their excellent book[4] on this topic, authors Jeffery Pfeffer and Robert I. Sutton give us great guidelines:

> 'One of the main barriers to turning knowledge into action is the tendency to treat talking about something as equivalent to actually doing something about it. Talking about what should be done, writing plans about what an organization should do, and collecting and analyzing data to help decide what actions to take can guide and motivate action. Indeed, rhetoric frequently is an essential first step toward taking action. But just talking about what to do isn't enough. Nor is planning for the future enough to produce that future. Something has to get done, and someone has to do it.'

With this quote in mind, allow me to walk us through what the Bible says about the transformative power of the Gospel. We know that the Gospel changes everything…. There is no sin, no problem in our lives and no obstacle so big that the Gospel cannot transform it. This process starts with God and God alone. The good news of Jesus starts with "in the beginning, God created the heavens and the earth."[5] God created everything, including us, and to understand the Gospel we start by understanding that God is

---

3. James 1:22
4. Pfeffer, Jeffery and Sutton, Robert I. The Knowing-Doing Gap: How Smart Companies Turn Knowledge into Action. Harvard Business School Press; 1st edition
5. Gen. 1:1

holy and righteous. Because of that, he is determined to not ever ignore or tolerate sin. We see that sin coming about shortly after God created the first human beings, and He intended for Adam and Eve to live in wonderful harmony under his righteous rule, obeying Him and living in fellowship with Him. Adam broke that fellowship with God as He ate the forbidden fruit, the one that God told him not to eat. In addition, Adam and Eve had instigated rebellion against God. It is at this part of the story that many people ask 'Why do pastors teach that I must face the consequences of Adam's sin when I didn't personally eat the fruit? In fact, I wasn't even there!' Paul gives us a succinct answer in Romans 5 when he writes, 'just as sin came into the world through one man, and death through sin, and so death spread to all men because all sinned.'

It was through Adam, then, that sin entered the world and from that point on, every person born inherits Adam's sin nature and suffers the same consequences of spiritual and physical death. Paul's famous verse in Romans on this topic comes to mind when he writes, 'for all have sinned and fall short of the glory of God.'[6]

At this point in the story, I must mention that in this sin and apart from the gospel, our human existence is hollow, and our future is hopeless. We try to fill that gospel-sized hole in our hearts with other things, but testimony after testimony indicates to us that we are unable to help ourselves out of this horrible situation. We are dead spiritually and hopeless without Christ. As you already know, the story doesn't end here. We all know the famous verses from John, "For God so loved the world, that he gave his only Son, that whoever believes in him should not perish but have eternal life. For God did not send his Son into the world to condemn the world, but in order that the world might be saved through him."[7] God sent His Son as a substitute for our sin! Paul tells us in Ephesians that, "God, being rich in mercy, because of the great love with which he loved us, even when we were dead in our trespasses, made us alive together with Christ—by grace you have been saved."[8] We all know about Jesus' substitutionary atonement, where Jesus died in our place for our sins when He was crucified on the cross. We are the ones who deserved to be placed on that cross to die, but Jesus took the punishment on Himself; that is, He substituted Himself for us and took the sin that is rightly ours—that we deserved. I love Paul's explanation of this substitution when he writes, "For

---

6. Romans 3:23
7. John 3:16-17
8. Ephesians 2:4-5

our sake he made him to be sin who knew no sin, so that in him we might become the righteousness of God."[9]

We get now to the really good news! Not only did Jesus give His life for us, he now offers us a 'bridge'[10] to a relationship with God and a life full of peace, love and joy. The Apostle Peter says it best in his first letter to the churches in modern-day Turkey, 'For Christ also suffered once for sins, the righteous for the unrighteous, that he might bring us to God, being put to death in the flesh but made alive in the spirit."[11] As we turn our lives over to Jesus and repent of our sins, we are new creations, able to live a life with Christ and for Christ. One of my favorite Scripture memory verses about this comes from 2 Corinthians. "Therefore, if anyone is in Christ, he is a new creation. The old has passed away; behold, the new has come. [18] All this is from God, who through Christ reconciled us to himself and gave us the ministry of reconciliation."[12] Praise God!

Our Belief about Jesus' Power

You may be wondering why I'm reviewing the Gospel story to a bunch of church leaders, elders and pastors–and are probably saying to yourself right now that you already know this story well. The reason I'm reviewing the Gospel here is to get to the meat of this chapter. You may have heard of the equation *Stated belief + actual practice = actual belief.* All church leaders will say that the transformative power of the Gospel in people's lives is real, but what would I see if I came to your church and began asking congregation members to tell me how they have seen that power in their own lives? Would I hear story after story about transformed lives after hearing the Gospel and turning their lives over to Jesus? Would they tell me that they hear and see from you a true belief in the transformative power of the Gospel? And what would I hear if I interviewed you about this topic?

I believe that a church that has a confident expectation of Gospel transformation starts with that expectation lived out by the elders and senior leadership. The interviews I would conduct would tell me a lot about what the elders believe on this topic, and no one at your church is going to confidently expect Gospel transformation until you as an elder or pastor believe it. As

---

9. 2 Corinthians 5:21
10. http://oneeightcatalyst.org/wp-content/uploads/2018/01/OEC-Bridge-Illustration.pdf
11. 1 Peter 3:18
12. 2 Corinthians 5:17-18

I tour churches, conducting these types of interviews and observing what is happening in churches that I visit, there is one main reason that this sort of gospel-centered transformation among the congregation doesn't happen. Simply put, it's a lack of belief in the Gospel and its true redemptive power at the pastor/elder level.

Putting Belief into Practice

To show you what I'm talking about, let's consider a scenario of what not only preaching the Gospel, but truly believing that the Gospel can and should transform people's lives looks like.

Ed Romero is a 32-year-old who has started attending the young-adult Thursday night meeting at your church. As you get to know him, he begins to tell you his story: "I thought I was achieving the American dream, but ended up having my whole world fall apart overnight," says Ed. "I had it all: the college degree, the sweet apartment, the successful career, and the girlfriend. But then sales started drying up at work, and my long-term relationship ended. Everything I idolized was falling apart. I was at a real low point when a friend invited me to your Thursday young-adult meeting. Throughout my life, I would treat God like a genie. I would pray for a particular thing and then I would promise God that I would read my Bible if He came through. On my first visit to the church's Thursday night group, I felt very uncomfortable. My involvement with women, drugs, porn and alcohol was not what God wanted for me, but my pride kept me from being confronted with that truth."

This is a very common first phase in a person's testimony. This describes who Ed was before Christ. Many times, I talk with people who know about the Bible, or at least have some familiarity with the Bible. In our churches, we love meeting these types of people because clearly God is at work, and He is getting ready to do something potentially big!

Ed continues, "So, rather than moving toward the Lord, whom I had known about my entire life, I jumped into another relationship. That relationship was extremely unhealthy, and the choices I made as it ended demonstrated just how depraved my heart was. My life was all about my needs, and I knew that was wrong, so I eventually took steps to return to the Lord. I was still partying Friday through Tuesday, then coming to the Thursday night group, but I found it exhausting to live in both worlds."

At this second stage, we must not only be telling folks like Ed that Jesus died for them and that Jesus wants to have a relationship with him, but also that Jesus wants to fundamentally transform their hearts and their minds. As Paul writes in Romans 2, 'Do not be conformed to this world, but be transformed by the renewal of your mind.'[13]

"After hearing a message on Matthew 7:15-18 about bearing good fruit," Ed continues, "I realized I was not the man I wanted to be, and that I was not producing any good fruit in my life. At home that Thursday night, I told God that I was sick and tired of being sick and tired. I surrendered everything – my life, my job, my relationships, my money – to the Lord because I was tired of running. That's the night I trusted my life to Christ and asked Him to take me, break me, and make me look more like Him."

As you hear Ed's story, your heart rejoices! At your church, you've seen God work mightily in Ed's life. You are so very happy about what is happening on Thursday nights, because clearly Ed was around people who love Jesus and had an influence on his life. You also are happy to know that the leaders in the Thursday night group were used to confront Ed with his sin and his need for Jesus.

"The Lord helped me change my playmates and playground. Soon I got connected and into community with other believers here at this church. I started serving in the children's ministry and started attending a Men's Tuesday night study. That's where the Lord placed more men in my life to help me grow. I met a Men's Ministry team leader, Billy, who taught me about what it meant to follow Christ. It was still a daily struggle against pride, perfectionism, and lust, but God used the men at my table at the study to hold me accountable. I learned the value of confession and repentance and was thankful for friends who encouraged me as I grew in Christ. Coworkers at my office have been asking me questions as they sense there is something different about my life. I now have conversations with workmates about finding my identity, not in what I owned or where I worked, but in the Lord. I don't have to work in fulltime ministry to be effective for Christ, I can have an impact right where I work now. The Lord slowly chipped away from the fleeting things I put my identity in and reminded me that nothing else will ever satisfy

---

13. Romans 12:2

the way Christ does." "I'm particularly thrilled with my volunteer work in the Children's ministry. Our lessons on godly character traits are just as relevant to adults as they are to fourth or fifth graders. When I was that age, I viewed God as a cosmic killjoy who kept me away from fun stuff! Our kids know that the Bible is a bunch of smaller stories that point to the one-big-true story of God's rescue plan of His people through the death, burial, and resurrection of His Son, Jesus. They also know that following Christ is the most fun adventure ever, and I have learned that right along with them! Today the kids I met when I first started volunteering in the fourth-grade class are now moving into junior high. Because I didn't follow Christ until I was a young adult, I have more scars from sin than these kids will ever have if they continue living faithfully with the Lord. My prayer is that they will understand that we have a Savior who loves us and offers us a better life than anything we could plan ourselves. It's a privilege to share that message with our next generation of leaders every week!"[14]

Ed's story is a great account of a fully transformed life because of the Gospel! And because we would define a disciple as someone who learns from Jesus how to live like Jesus — someone who, because of God's awakening grace, conforms his or her own words and ways to the words and ways of Jesus. A disciple of Jesus wants to learn from Him, through the study of God's Word, the Bible, and as we listen to others teach from it, we would say that it is not only when friends like Ed hear the Gospel that they become a disciple, but also those who are walking with him in his faith journey and help him get to a point where the Gospel fully transforms his everything. And in Ed's story, we see the process of 2 Timothy 2:2, which is well known as *the* verse in relation to making disciples, played out to completion, "what you have heard from me in the presence of many witnesses entrust to faithful men, who will be able to teach others also." The Gospel message was communicated to Ed, his life was transformed, and he then was able to teach others about the Gospel and its transformation!

Spreading a Confident Expectation of God's Work

So how can you begin to change the culture at your church to one that

---

14. Ed's story, with major changes, is loosely based from a story from https://www.watermark. org/blog/stories

carries a confident expectation of God's ability to work 'miracles' in the lives of your congregation? As I've been thinking and praying about what tips to give you, an article by Chuck Lawless on www.thomrainer.com came to my mind. Chuck, whom I've interviewed for a podcast episode, is the Dean of Doctoral Studies and Vice-President of Spiritual Formation and Ministry Centers at Southeastern Seminary in Wake Forest, NC, where he also serves as Professor of Evangelism and Missions. The article is titled, *'Why Churches Talk The Great Commission But Don't Do It.'*[15] I've used the article as a reference many times as I'm talking about Great Commission fulfillment in the local church, and I think many of the principles he's talking about in this article apply here as well. Chuck lists nine reasons why many churches talk about the Great Commission but don't do it, and while I won't go through all nine, many of them are quite apropos! In his first point, he writes, "Church leaders talk the language without letting the biblical texts "sink in." This is true for the confident expectation I'm writing about here as well. Do you as a church leader at your church talk about God's power to change lives in a Sunday School Class or Sunday Sermon, but don't believe in your heart that God can and will change even the 'worst' of sinners?

Chuck also writes that when it comes to Great Commission fulfillment in churches, many times pastors themselves are not committed to this task: 'I cannot say these words strongly enough, however: I have never seen a Great Commission church led by a pastor who was not himself deeply committed to the task. Unless a pastor bleeds for his neighbors and the nations to know Christ, the church he leads will not live out this burden.'

Similarly, I've not seen a church that is actively seeing God at work in amazing ways in a church where the pastor doesn't believe that God is able to do amazing things. This comes through in your preaching and in the way the leaders talk at your church. Dr. Lawless also states that some leaders settle for partial obedience to the Great Commission. You may find yourself knowing mentally that God is able to do big things and everywhere you read in the Bible, you're seeing Bible passages like we read in Deuteronomy 10, For the LORD your God is God of gods and Lord of lords, the great, the mighty, and the awesome God....'[16], so you say with your lips, 'Yes, God is great and mighty and able to do big things,' but as people look at how that's applied to your life and ministry, they are left to wonder.

---

15. https://thomrainer.com/2014/06/churches-talk-great-commission-dont/
16. Deuteronomy 10:17

What's my point on how this can be applied in your life and in your ministry at your church? Through your preaching, your teaching and training, your counseling and by how you act and what you say when talking to people about God's ability to change lives, you not only know mentally about this power that God has, it *must* ooze out of you in all you say or do. Whether you're talking to the drug-addicted, broke single mother with AIDS, or the financial well-off CEO who seems to have it all but is dying inside, your message stays the same: Through Jesus, you can find life, and a whole new abundant life! It doesn't matter what you have done or where you been, Jesus came to set the captives free! And I believe that message rings particularly clear through church leaders who can cite the many ways in which God has transformed their own hearts and minds and are openly willing to share what God is continuing to do in their lives.

Another way that you can begin to lead a shift in your church culture in this way is by writing down and sharing stories of people at your church whose lives have been transformed. Through the church blog, video testimonies given on a Sunday morning and then posted on the church website, and even having those people come up for a ten-minute testimony on a Sunday morning are all great ways. This emphasis begins to show that the leadership is saying 'We are serious about Gospel transformation at our church,' and reinforces what you're saying to others. Highlighting these stories is key! I believe that this culture shift strongly aids in making disciples of Jesus, because the one who has been set free from sin and bondage becomes fully-devoted to Jesus and then wants to tell others their story of what Jesus has done in his or her life.

I pray that you catch a vision for this transformative culture shift at your church!

Discussion Questions

1. As you and your team assess how you are doing at communicating the full transformative power of the Gospel to your congregation, what does that assessment look like?

2. If an interview team were to quiz your congregation regarding what they understand about the transformative power of the Gospel, what would they hear? Are you willing to ask those questions?

3. As you read Ed Romero's story, do you know a lot of the stories of people at your own church whose lives God has changed? If not, why not?

4. What shifts do you think you may need to make in your culture to embrace a confident expectation of the transformative power of the Gospel? As you identify these potential shifts, what concrete steps can you take to begin that process?

4

The Third Mark of a Church that Makes Disciples

A Continual Commitment to Equipping Through Training

Throughout the course of our lives, we have all heard stories of people who have chosen to pursue excellence in their field of expertise. Some of my own favorites have come from listening to the annual Pro Football Hall of Fame inductees' speeches. Having made it to the pinnacle of their sport, these men often talk about their love of the game and their passion to be the best, stating their commitment that no one would ever outwork them on the field or in their study of the game. Mike Ditka, a National Football League player for eleven years, and later the coach of three different NFL teams (including the 1985 Super Bowl champion Chicago Bears) was inducted into the Hall of Fame in 1988. In his induction speech, Ditka said, 'In life, many men have talent. But talent in itself is no accomplishment. Excellence in football and excellence in life is bred when men recognize their opportunities and then pursue them with a passion.'[1] The Third Mark of a Church that Makes Disciples is a church that pursues, with passion, the equipping through training of its congregation. A congregation that is receiving regular training and equipping becomes a church whose leaders are constantly 'giving away' the ministry to the congregation. If you as a pastor want to 'get in the game' of creating a church that makes disciples, I invite you to think with me about what this Mark looks like and why it's important. The local church needs

---

1. https://www.youtube.com/watch?v=pSqdRMi3TNw

pastors that are full of God-given passion and who want to become experts at guiding their churches to becoming disciple-making churches. Doing this work will require everything you've got, but it's worth the effort, and the community where your church is located is waiting for you to come and tell them about Jesus.

Equipping those in your congregation is a key step toward becoming an effective disciple-making church. Can we agree at this point in the book that becoming specialists at being and making disciples is one of the main purposes God has for the local church? J.D. Greear, president of the Southern Baptist Convention, wrote recently that 'everything we do in ministry should flow from or lead toward making disciples. Disciple-making is, after all, the key component of Jesus's Great Commission[2], and it ought to be the standard by which we judge every ministry in the church.'[3] Given my years of study, experience and research on what the local church should be doing, I couldn't agree more! So, if God is calling His local churches to be making disciples, shouldn't we become experts at making disciples? Especially given what we've already covered about the 'awake at 3am' biblical responsibility that you have as an overseer of your local church! Remember, you're charged with watching over the flock that Jesus paid for with his own blood and watching over their souls! God wants you as an elder or pastor to be excellent at making disciples!

Becoming an Expert at Something

If the target is to become an expert at making disciples at your church, how is that accomplished? An honest assessment in clarifying what you currently know about making disciples is a great first step. You are probably closer than you think at being an expert at making disciples, especially since you are studious in your daily reading and study of God's Word. As I often say as I'm speaking about this topic, anyone who is reading his or her Bible on a regular basis sees all throughout the New Testament the verses that fuel being and making disciples. You have read Paul's admonition to young Timothy for him to do his best to 'present yourself to God as one approved, a worker who has no need to be ashamed,

---

2. Matthew 28:19-20
3. https://www.imb.org/2019/07/22/make-disciples/

rightly handling the Word of Truth.'[4] I am sure you want each member in your congregation to be able to rightly handle the Bible. Later in that same letter to Timothy, Paul encourages Timothy to 'preach the Word; be ready in season and out of season; reprove, rebuke, and exhort, with complete patience and teaching.'[5] I'm sure that as you've thought about those you lead, you know that most of them will not be able to be ready at all times to preach the Word to others without your help in teaching them how to do it. As I write this chapter, I am trying my best to draw out of you that heart you once had or still must get laser sharp on your responsibilities as a shepherd of your flock.

As I tap into that focus on those you lead, much of what I've learned about becoming an expert at anything requires that you must have a passion for the topic on which you want to be an expert. It must resonate with every fiber of who you are! I can tell you from experience that, once you start helping people to grow spiritually and find a love for God's Word on their own, the result for you will be a fueled passion to do more of it!

Once you assess what you know about making disciples, continued study is the next step. Obviously, since you are reading this book, either on your own or with your church's senior leadership team, you are on the right path! This step leads right into the third step at becoming an expert. A lot of work and dedication must go into examining all the steps needed to make your church one that makes disciples. Reading books, taking online courses, watching videos and lots and lots of time with your leadership team in God's Word, discussing Bible passages and how you all will put those passages into practice.

As you implement the Six Marks of a Church that Makes Disciples in this book, and as you find additional material, you'll experience some trial and error. You may be familiar with the oft-quoted Malcom Gladwell who, in his book, *Outliers: The Story of Success*, reported from his research that it takes about 10,000 hours of practice to achieve mastery in a particular field. Other sources have pushed back on the 10,000 hours generality. Regardless if 10,000 hours is exactly how many hours of practice it takes to become an expert at something, the point is still poignant: think about each of these Six Marks and begin practicing and perfecting these principles for that many hours. I am truly calling you to invest the hours with your people in your

---

4. 2 Timothy 2:15
5. Timothy 4:2

congregation. In this journey, define what keeps you from wanting to be excellent at making disciples, and put those barriers at the feet of the cross to be crucified forever! You will develop a quiet confidence as you settle on the biblical imperative given to you through Scripture to make disciples of Jesus every day, and it will rub off on those in your congregation.

Making Disciples through Equipping through Training

As I get-laser focused myself on helping you begin to think through how you can best equip your congregation through training, there are three steps I feel compelled to cover with you. First, let's look exactly what *Equipping through Training* is; then we'll look at some practical first steps for equipping your congregation through training, and finally, we'll look at some of the long-term benefits of keeping a commitment to equipping through training are for the long-term future of your church.

The dictionary definition is a useful starting point for understanding what equipping really is. Merriam-Webster offers two definitions for the word *equip* and I think they are both useful: 'to furnish for service or action by appropriate provisioning' and 'to make ready: prepare.'[6] Both of these definitions give us a good start. To equip people means to give them all they need before taking action and making sure they are prepared. We often see this word used in a variety of situations.

- College students get equipped in their classes for their job field and life after college.
- Airlines have pilot development offices to equip their pilots, not only for an initial job with their company, but also for continual training on new aircraft and refresher training.
- A firefighter goes through fire academy training to become equipped to safely fight fires and save lives. We would never imagine a firefighter showing up to the scene of a fire without the proper training! That could result in a deadly disaster! We see this same pattern as it relates to church leaders equipping their congregation for everything they need, both for their own walks with Christ, and for a lifetime of ministry. It is one of the key ways I believe elders

---

6. https://www.merriam-webster.com/dictionary/equip

fulfill the 'awake at 3am' verses and their biblical duties.

Biblically, we see several imperatives given to church leaders for equipping their congregation. The most famous of the passages is in Ephesians 4. It's a long passage, but one that deserves a few minutes of our time. The apostle Paul writes,

> 'And he gave the apostles, the prophets, the evangelists, the shepherds and teachers, *to equip the saints for the work of ministry,* for building up the body of Christ, until we all attain to the unity of the faith and of the knowledge of the Son of God, to mature manhood, to the measure of the stature of the fullness of Christ, so that we may no longer be children, tossed to and fro by the waves and carried about by every wind of doctrine, by human cunning, by craftiness in deceitful schemes. Rather, speaking the truth in love, we are to *grow up in every way into him who is the head, into Christ,* from whom the whole body, joined and held together by every joint with which it is equipped, when each part is working properly, makes the body grow so that it builds itself up in love.'[7] (italics mine.)

In this text, Paul first gives us a clear answer to who should be doing the equipping: apostles (the church planters of the day), prophets (the theological truth tellers), evangelists, the shepherds (that's you, Pastor!) and the teachers. To me, that looks like a list of what the qualities of a church leader looks like.

For those church leaders reading this now, it seems like the job of equipping the saints is yours to do. I'm also interested in what the end result of the equipping is for the work of ministry and the building up of the body. Here we find a key component. As church leaders are equipping, you're building up people to do ministry themselves and helping them become mature Christians.

As I think about equipping your people for the work of ministry and to grow up in Christ, there's one specific passage of Scripture that stays in my mind as a starting point for your ministry of equipping through training. This passage of Scripture includes a particularly famous verse, one that is likely one of the most memorized verses in all of the Bible.

> 'But as for you, continue in what you have learned and have firmly believed, knowing from whom you learned it and how from childhood

---

7. Ephesians 4:11-16

you have been acquainted with the sacred writings, which are able to make you wise for salvation through faith in Christ Jesus. All Scripture is breathed out by God and profitable for teaching, for reproof, for correction, and for training in righteousness, that the man of God may be complete, equipped for every good work.'[8]

Paul first instructs us to continue in what we have learned and firmly believed. This indicates that we are using knowledge, experience and education that we've already received and have now put into practice. He then points to the one place that equipping through training should come from: The Bible. Our Bible is profitable for us in at least four areas, according to this passage, and I believe that Paul put the four areas here in their particular order for a particular reason.

As you're walking people through equipping through training, first comes teaching from Scripture. Whole books have been written on this topic but suffice it to say that all of our equipping through training should be biblically based. This teaching leads to reproof, which can be thought of as a reprimand or rebuke, as our lives are held up to the light of biblical teaching. After the reproof comes correction, as we make a course correction to fall in line with biblical teaching. I often think of 1 Timothy 6 in this regard. As Paul is listing his way through all the evils of the world, he zeros in on the love of money being the root of all evil. His course correction? 'But as for you, O man of God, flee (literally 'escape quickly') these things. Pursue righteousness, godliness, faith, love, steadfastness, gentleness.'[9]

Finally, after the teaching, the reproof and correction, we have training in righteousness. Any equipping through training that you do with your church needs to come through the Bible. Train your people to know God's Word, how to handle it and read it and use it correctly. The righteousness that has come to believers in Christ will come to fruition by the training through God's Word. What is the result in this passage of equipping through God's Word? That people of God may be complete, equipped for every good work.

Worried how you're going to truly begin to fulfill the 'awake at 3am' verses? Make your people complete and give them the tools for every good work. Help them know how to handle the Bible, how to use it to make a defense for their faith and how to share the Gospel using God's Word as

---

8. 2 Timothy 2:14-17
9. 1 Timothy 6:11

their guide. If you've ever known someone who has a thorough knowledge of the Bible and knows how to use it correctly, you know what I am talking about here. These are the 'Stephens' in our midst, people who are 'full of faith and of the Holy Spirit.' This completeness can be mightily used by God in His kingdom work! Imagine your congregation with a growing number of these 'complete' people, better able to help you and join with you in the ministry that God has given you and the elders of your church! Church leader, this maturity begins with you getting 'complete,' then having a commitment, as Paul did, as he instructed Timothy that 'what you have heard from me in the presence of many witnesses entrust to faithful men, who will be able to teach others also.'[10]

First Steps toward Building a Culture of Equipping through Training

As I write this book, one of the issues that I wrestle with in is how to help churches who are not currently seeing many of these *Marks of a Church that Makes Disciples* go from inaction to action. I wrestle with the shock that it may bring to congregations who have become comfortable with the 'status quo,' and in fact, this current mode of operating is probably why many are going to your church. As I was seeking counsel from a new friend who is a leader at a church that has done almost all of this really well, I asked him what advice he would have for those who will read this book and who are also wrestling with this same question. His answer surprised me, although it made sense the more I've had a chance to think on it. His advice simply was this: 'Mike, if these church elders feel compelled to do their absolute best to obey what you've been calling the 'awake at 3am' verses, they must simply explain to their people that, in order for them to obey what God has called them to do as elders and to oversee the flock in the absolute best way, these Marks need to be implemented immediately without any slow roll out.' His answer will resonate with us throughout the rest of this book because it has applicability throughout the rest of this volume.

But some of you may need to invest some time to think through what that really means. In this case of Equipping through Training, my simple suggestion would be to begin to offer a few classes, maybe one night

---

10. 2 Timothy 2:2

a week, taught initially by elders and pastors. Later, you will hopefully have a growing number of 'Stephens' who will feel led to take on the responsibility.

Here are a few suggestions as to some initial class offerings that would help your people to become 'complete:'

'What is a Disciple of Jesus?': The first book in this 'Six Marks' book series is a book I wrote called *What You Do Shows Who You Are: The Six Marks of a Disciple of Jesus.* This is a great starting point to help your people begin to wrestle with and find victory in their walk with Jesus. Designed as an eight-week course, the book reads more like a workbook, with eight questions at the end of every chapter that will encourage discussion in its intended small group environment. A class like this is a good *'Christianity 101'* kind of class, which helps people begin talking and helping each other in areas where they may struggle. The book is available on www.amazon.com or by calling our ministry offices.

Basic Spiritual Disciplines: A great place to start with your congregation is to introduce them to the basic disciplines that will transform their walk with Christ. I often call these Spiritual Disciplines, such as how to have a quiet time, how to begin Scripture Memory, how to read the Bible, etc. These disciplines help believers begin to have a daily walk with Jesus. The training then continues to deeper content needed for a growing relationship with God. These might include classes in how to share your faith and your testimony, and how to properly interpret Scripture.

From Front to Back: Understanding the Story of the Bible from Genesis to Revelation: This type of course begins to give people an understanding of the structure, timeline, and major themes of Scripture. I love these types of 'overview' classes, because I find that most people in our churches have never read all the way through the Bible, and showing them that there is relevance to our daily lives throughout Scripture, from beginning to end, is key. This class also backs up the first of our *Marks* in this book in that it helps you emphasize the importance of all of God's Word.

Ask Any Question: A Safe Place to explore the Christian faith: This would be probably taught by a senior leader who has a very good handle on scriptural knowledge. This is such a key class today because, to a recent Gallup poll, only 24% of Americans believe that the Bible is the literal Word of God. Interestingly, the same Gallup poll also found that almost three-quarters of Americans continue to see the Bible as a holy document and believe that it is God-inspired if not God's own words.[11]

This may be a great class to offer to the community-at-large to introduce them to your church. The people around you have a high view of the Bible, and this may be a way to show them that it is also God-inspired.

As you begin to form a "we do this every Thursday night" type of groove on the church calendar, and you begin to have more and more 'Stephens,' there is almost no limit to the kinds of one-day training sessions you could do on Saturdays, or maybe Sundays after church. The topics of these sessions could be topics from the fields of apologetics, Bible interpretation, theology, current events, practical life skills, spiritual growth, and evangelism, each of which could be featured a couple of times a year. I love this because now you're really beginning to teach and lead on several levels, and certainly you're doing your best to obey Paul's admonition to Timothy as he encourages him to '**Do your best** to present yourself to God as one approved, a worker who has no need to be ashamed, rightly handling the Word of Truth.'[12]

Men's and Women's Studies: Being able to fold in your existing Men's and Women's studies into 'Equipping through Training' is a great way to show your people that when we come together, the study and implementation of God's word is what we're about. With the additional training opportunities that you develop, maybe the Men's and Women's studies are times to do a book of the Bible study in an expositional fashion, detailing and pulling out the meaning of the particular text or passage of Scripture, then talking about it in the group.

---

11. https://news.gallup.com/poll/210704/record-few-americans-believe-bible-literal-word-god.aspx
12. 2 Timothy 2:15

Wrapping It Up: Why This Is So Important

As we close out this chapter, you can see how offering these classes helps you as an elder to do your best as you watch over your people's souls and help them present themselves to God as a worker able to handle God's Word well. It also helps you meet several of the Marks that I've already mentioned in this book. Let me show you what I'm talking about.

One of my favorite Scripture passages of all time is 1 Peter 3:15. Peter is addressing the churches in modern day Turkey, and he writes, 'but in your hearts honor Christ the Lord as holy, always being prepared to make a defense to anyone who asks you for a reason for the hope that is in you; yet do it with gentleness and respect.' This verse contains three parts. The second part is our focus at this point. This verse gives us a biblical command to 'always be prepared to make a defense to anyone who asks you for a reason for the hope that is in you.' The command includes a definitive time period ('always'), it gives us the action ('make a defense'), and to whom, ('anyone'), and a defense of 'the reason for the hope that is in you.' So, when you offer an annual 'How to share your faith' class to your congregation and advertise attending the class is an expectation, you're actually accomplishing multiple marks of a church that makes disciples at one time! You are saying 'If the Bible says it, then we do it' (we are all about making a defense) and therefore promoting a high view of Scripture. You are also saying that you have confidence that God can use each member of your congregation in the lives of their neighbors, friends and workmates ("we have an expectation that as you, congregation member, share your defense, we have an expectation about what God can do in that person's life").

As I hope you have had the opportunity to experience as well, whenever I've given a 'defense for the reason for the hope that is in me,' my life and walk with Jesus are impacted too! As a side note, think conversely about what you are communicating to your congregation if you *don't* offer this training class. "Yes, I know Scripture teaches that we should all know how to give a defense to anyone who asks us the reason for the hope that is in us, but I don't really want to go to that much effort to teach you about this." Awake at 3am, much? You are saying a lot about what you think of Scripture, what you think about the command given to you as an elder to watch over the flock and to watch over their souls. As you ponder this topic, also remember the biblical instruction we've already looked at in this chapter that 'all Scripture is breathed out by God and profitable for teaching, for reproof, for correction, and for training in righteousness, that the man of God may be complete, equipped for every good work.'[13] All of Scripture, breathed out by God, is profitable for teaching and training, so that God's people will be equipped for anything life throws at them.

May God be with you as you wrestle with how to best equip your congregation through training. As we read in the benediction of the book of Hebrews, 'Now may the God of peace who brought again from the dead our Lord Jesus, the great shepherd of the sheep, by the blood of the eternal covenant, *equip you with everything good that you may do his will*, working in us that which is pleasing in his sight, through Jesus Christ, to whom be glory forever and ever. Amen.'[14]

Discussion Questions

1. As you assess your church leadership team (senior staff and elders), what is the level of commitment and passion to leading your church to become excellent at being and making disciples? If that passion is lacking, what could you all do, in practical terms, to (re)kindle that pursuit with passion?

---

13. 2 Timothy 3:16-17
14. Hebrews 13:20-21

2. Do you agree with Southern Baptist Convention President J.D. Greear's quote that "everything we do in ministry should flow from or lead toward making disciples. Disciple making is, after all, the key component of Jesus's Great Commission, and it ought to be the standard by which we judge every ministry in the church." As you use disciple- making as the standard to judge the various ministries of your church, what ministries 'pass the test,' and which ones could use work?

3. How is your church's culture moving toward equipping through training? In what areas do you need a 'refresh' and which areas could use a whole new plan?

4. As you look at the list of *Equipping through Training* course suggestions, which topics could you start to implement now, and which ones would you like to emphasize over the next year? Do you have a pipeline of 'Stephens' ready to help you teach? If not, what steps could be taken to begin to fill the pipeline?

5

The Fourth Mark of a Church that Makes Disciples

Discovering the Redemptive Power of Community

I can remember the day that I felt God definitively pulling my heart toward reaching the Chinese for Christ. I was on my first 'vision trip' in 1996, a six-week affair that pulled my heart in several directions. On the second full day of the trip, I was sitting at a table on a sidewalk eating a bowl of noodles with one of the team leaders for the trip, a man who had already lived in China for a few years. I sorely miss the mid-1990's Chinese cities, where anyplace was open for any kind of commercial activity, as it was on this day. Our "noodle shop" was a guy who had mounted cooking pots on his three-wheeled bike, and a few small tables and chairs he had whipped out on a sidewalk where his customers could sit and enjoy his noodles.

As the team leader and I sat on the sidewalk on a hot summer day, he and I enjoyed each other's company—in the July heat, eating our hot bowls of noodles and drinking Coke from bottles, which was the only way you could drink Coke in China in those days! Suddenly, a very large fly flew into my noodles and embedded itself in the noodle concoction. At this point, I had a decision to make: Did I believe that the fly had ruined my noodles, as many Americans might think? Without skipping a beat, I confidently picked up my chopsticks, fished around for the fly, found and grabbed the fly and promptly flicked it to the sidewalk, and kept eating my noodles without any commentary about the fly itself. Of course, the team leader, who was also an American and watching all of this, looked down at his own bowl of noodles, as if to contemplate what he would have done with the fly. Then he looked up at me and said, 'Mike, you were made for this place!'

At that moment, I felt God say to my heart in a small, still voice, *'Yes, Mike, I did make you for this place.'*

This newfound call to China meant that I needed to begin learning how to read and speak Chinese. One of the realities of doing ministry in China is that very few people in China speak any English, even to this day. You cannot even leave your arrival airport in China without either knowing the Chinese language yourself or being with someone who does know Chinese, because none of the taxi or bus drivers know any English! So, upon my arrival back home from my first trip to China, I began the process of learning Chinese.

For native English speakers, learning Chinese poses a real challenge because it is so very different from English. The subscription-based language learning app and E-learning platform, *Babbel,* had recently rated the hardest languages for native English speakers to learn. Chinese was rated as the #1 hardest language for English speakers to learn, even ahead of languages like Arabic, Polish and Russian![1]

As I learned over the four years that followed that initial trip to China, Chinese is so difficult for native English speakers to learn for several key reasons. The first challenge is the tonal nature of Chinese. There are four tones in Chinese, so depending on the tone you put on a word, it can have different meanings. As an example, consider the Chinese word 'ma.' Depending on the tone you put on this word, it can mean "mother," "horse," "rough" or "scold!"

The other very difficult part of learning Chinese is the picture-based character system it requires for writing. There is no alphabet in Chinese, so in order to learn to read, I had to memorize all the characters and their meaning! This means that there is no 'sounding out' words! In order to become fluent in Mandarin Chinese, one must memorize 3,000 characters out of the 7,000 total, some of which are now rarely used. So, over the course of about six years, I began learning Chinese through tutors, Chinese classes at an

---

1. https://www.babbel.com/en/magazine/6-hardest-languages-for-english-speakers-to-learn/

American University, and living in China doing full-time language study for thirteen months. My experience is that, yes, learning the language is as hard as everyone says it is, but I also remember the gradual steps I took in language study and how fun it was to slowly be able to communicate with Chinese friends with increasing confidence!

One of my real language 'victories' occurred early in our time of living in China. I remember how the signs above the shops and restaurants in the city where we lived seemed to come alive! Where once they were incomprehensible 'babble,' I could now recognize the bakery apart from the SiChuan style restaurant, and the pharmacy from the bank! I could actually *read* the signs! As I look back now at all the hard work that learning Chinese required for me, still it pales in comparison to the nine million Chinese Bibles we've been able to distribute, the multiple churches we've helped to start and build in rural China, and all the other projects God has allowed us to accomplish--in large part because of my ability to communicate with the Chinese in their own language. Whatever problem needed to be solved or meetings needed to be held for our ministry, I could confidently lead and participate in those meetings using Chinese.

The Fourth Mark of a Church that Makes Disciples is the true redemptive power of community. While many Churches have small groups, Sunday School classes and other similar communities meeting together, I'm afraid that many churches have begun a disciple-making resource that seems and remains incomplete. Here's what you'll find about community that aids in making disciples: much like Americans learning how to speak Chinese, the experience of community is really hard to do well at first, but over time, the fruit that is borne by learning and practicing it well makes it no longer a burden, but transforms it into a blessing.

As you shepherd and pay careful attention to your flock in your role as an overseer, developing a true community ministry structure is one of the absolute best ways to accomplish what God calls you to do through His Word. If you truly believe that God has called you to shepherd your congregation and watch over their souls, this will be a great tool for you to use. As a ministry leader with a long history of community group participation, I begin by sharing with you what my experience in small group ministry has been.

Because of my interest in effective ministry models, I have paid particular attention to the structure of the small group ministries I've participated in during my thirty-two years of church participation. I have been involved in three or four different church-based small groups, and all have had a similar feel and structure. I would be placed into a small group generally with others who fit my stage in life, whether that be singles, young marrieds, marrieds with small children, etc. After an initial meeting to get to know the others I'd been paired with and we'd chosen the general theme of our study--and in at least one case—it was only a 'dinner and prayer' group. I think every 'Community' group I've been a part of has met together once a month, with occasional men's or women's only events (going to a ball game for the guys and "girls' night out" types of events for the gals.) The training for the leaders was minimal, outside of questions like, "Are you a Christian?" and "Are you interested in being a small group leader?" If I could answer 'Yes' to these questions, I would be invited and encouraged to come to a one-time training meeting the following week. I cannot recall any of the small groups I've been a part of that had a central purpose or theme communicated as to why we were meeting in this way, outside of a general sense that this is just what churches do.

I'd like to present a new model for your church in the area of Community that will lead people toward spiritual growth and becoming a fully devoted follower of Jesus. This model for Community at your church will help you build small groups that have purpose and meaning, and you'll see spiritual growth happening within the groups as well as members encouraging and praying for one another. You'll see confession of sin, and that sin beginning to fall away in people's lives, people earnestly praying for one another and taking on burdens, and both life and peace increasing in the lives of the people within each of the small groups at your church.

If this outcome is one you'd like to see in your church and if it would help you keep watch over the souls of those in your congregation, please allow me to lay out for you what that can look like at your church.

The Structure

As you imagine what a disciple-making community ministry could look like at your church, let's first address the structure needed to make it work. Fortunately, Exodus 18 gives us a great model to follow.

In this story, Jethro, who was Moses' Father-in-law, comes for a visit, together with Moses' wife Zipporah and their two sons. As Jethro sees how busy Moses is with his responsibilities in serving as a judge for all the people, Jethro makes a suggestion. Seeing Moses on his way toward spiritual burnout, he suggests,

> 'look for able men from all the people, men who fear God, who are trustworthy and hate a bribe, and place such men over the people as chiefs of thousands, of hundreds, of fifties, and of tens. And let them judge the people at all times. Every great matter they shall bring to you, but any small matter they shall decide themselves. So it will be easier for you, and they will bear the burden with you. If you do this, God will direct you, you will be able to endure, and all this people also will go to their place in peace."[2]

In this passage, we see a very familiar organizational structure, one that has been replicated millions of times over the course of human history: 'chiefs of thousands, of hundreds, of fifties, and of tens.' In this biblical structure, because the elders want to keep watch well and oversee the flock, they are the 'chiefs of thousands.' The next two levels can flex a bit given the size of the church and may either be paid staff or lay leaders, but you definitely want to have 'chiefs of hundreds and fifties.' You can have some fun determining who, within the staff structure and your key lay leaders, will fill these rolls. If you have a Community or Discipleship Pastor on staff, they would be the 'chiefs of hundreds,' and would be directly responsible for communicating to the elders, potentially writing up a monthly or weekly summary for the elders of what has happened in the community groups over the past week or month. This report would include victories (a wife of a couple in the group is fighting cancer and the community group is rallying around them to persevere, watching their children as needed and providing meals and biblical encouragement) and the stories where victory is elusive (the dad and father who is sleeping with prostitutes and is addicted to porn). This type of report would help you as an elder know the condition of the souls you're responsible for.

Reporting to the 'chief of hundreds' would be a 'chief of fifties,' which may be a community group director who is responsible for training and caring for community group leaders, who serve as the 'chiefs of ten.' This person might easily be a lay leader, who understands what you're doing in this ministry and is 'all in' on the vision behind it. In this structure, vision for the groups can easily move up and down the chain, as can the reports on how the groups are doing and what the groups are needing. With this structure, you're also fulfilling Paul's admonition to Timothy that 'what you've heard from me in the presence of many witnesses entrust to faithful men, who will be able to teach others also.'[3] You will want to develop faithful men (and women) up and down the line.

What do these groups look like in real terms?

Perhaps you are organizing your hierarchy and you're ready to either start small groups or to make adjustments to the groups you already must ensure that they are 'disciple-making' small groups. In my research of the churches that do this well, I've found six Core Values that these churches emphasize in each of their groups. These six Core Values lead to three questions that are asked each time a group meets together. I offer these here as a 'blueprint' for you to use as you see fit.

Community Core Value #1: Abide Daily

The very first value for a disciple-making community group is that each of its members should be working hard on his or her own relationship with Jesus and abiding in Him daily. We see this admonition in John 15 as Jesus states, 'I am the vine; you are the branches. Whoever abides in me and I in him, he it is that bears much fruit, for apart from me you can do nothing.' The most important action each member of the group can take to have a successful community group is to grow a healthy relationship with Christ.

---

3. 2 Timothy 2:2

We don't often use the word 'abide' in any other context than for our relationship with Christ. The English word 'abide' is the Greek word *meno*, which means 'to remain in' or 'to stay in.' The implication I get from this is that Jesus wants us to become like Him. As each member is becoming more like Christ in their individual walk with Jesus, it leads to a healthier community overall. Jesus reiterates this point in Matthew 6 as He states, 'But seek first the kingdom of God and his righteousness, and all these things will be added to you.'[4] Areas of focus to help each community group member would include daily time in the Bible, in prayer, and surrendering individual areas of sin to Christ and praising God as one sees Him working in great ways.

From the leader of the community group down the line to each member, we cannot be encouraging people to pursue Christ if we aren't doing so ourselves first. Paul knew this principle so well. In Philippians 4, he encourages the church at Philippi, 'What you have learned and received and heard and seen in me—practice these things, and the God of peace will be with you.'[5] Each community group will thrive when each person is thriving with Jesus!

Community Core Value #2: Be Devoted to One Another

The second Core Value for these community groups is an intentionality toward being absolutely committed to making the community group everything God intends it to be. The best way to do this is by going out of our way to demonstrate to the other people in the group that we are going to outdo all others in our commitment to the relationships created within the group. As we read in Romans 12, 'Love one another with brotherly affection. Outdo one another in showing honor.'[6] This Core Value may be the most difficult and take the most effort for a couple of key reasons. My extensive research and experience have shown me that we cannot be a good community if we meet only once a month in a 'supper club' style group to swap information. The effective disciple-making group will increasingly intertwine their lives with each other, and it's my deep conviction that the biblical community group will meet at least once a week.

If you are eating or drinking something while you read this, I'm sorry

4. Matthew 6:33
5. Philippians 4:9
6. Romans 12:10

for causing your 'spit take!' I understand that everyone is busy these days, and the last thing I would want to do is to add to your busyness. But I guarantee you that if you will mandate that the community groups at your church meet once a week, it'll change everything. There are several reasons why: First, Scripture clearly mandates it. As we read in the book of Hebrews, "Take care, brothers, lest there be in any of you an evil, unbelieving heart, leading you to fall away from the living God. But exhort one another **every day**, as long as it is called 'today,' that none of you may be hardened by the deceitfulness of sin."[7] I have found it extremely hard to 'exhort one another every day' if my group only sees each other one night a month for a shared meal!

Why are we mandated in Scripture to meet together every day? Our hearts, which are 'Prone to wander, Lord, I feel it, Prone to leave the God I love,'[8] tend to lead us away from God, and we need the exhortation daily to keep on track with our relationship with God. If the community groups meet weekly, with members checking in with each other daily with victories, prayer requests and 'oh boy, I really messed up, will you stand with me' messages, growth happens as each member is exhorting the other members to be the person of God they want and have committed to being. I have found it awfully difficult to 'Bear one another's burdens, and so fulfill the law of Christ'[9] when I'm only as aware of your current burdens as you are mine because we only meet one hour a month! The second reason that meeting weekly will change everything for the spiritual health of your small groups is that, if you believe that in order to shepherd the flock among you, you need to know how the 'sheep' are doing and that they are accounted for and cared for (remember the 'awake at 3am' verses), I think we would each agree that it's hard to account for and to know whose soul you're looking after if they are not a part of a shepherding structure. As we'll continue to see in this chapter, if they are just coming on Sunday morning and aren't a part of a shepherding structure, that doesn't say much about our shepherding because if people can come and go without any kind of life change, confession of sin, coming under the counsel of the church, and encouragement and equipping toward spiritual growth, your Hebrews 13 speech will lack detail.

7. Hebrews 3:12-13
8. Robert Robinson, "Come Thou Fount of Every Blessing"
9. Galatians 6:2

Community Group Weekly Question #1

Because these six Core Values can be hard for people to memorize, I believe that there are three questions that each leader can ask of each member that encapsulates the spirit of the six Core Values. To really see how people are doing in abiding well with Jesus, and giving/receiving exhortation, the leader can ask, **'How have you fed your soul?'** Answering this question will give people an opportunity to share with all how they experienced time with Jesus over the last week as well as the quality of time they had with other believers in giving encouragement and receiving admonishment.

Community Core Value #3: Living Authentically

In our churches today, it seems far too easy to come and go without revealing much about our lives and leaving large swaths of our lives hidden from sight. Yet we read throughout the Bible many examples of how letting our brothers and sisters know where we are in our lives in an increasingly trusting and authentic relationship brings life. Look at this passage from 1 John:

> 'But if we walk in the light, as he is in the light, we have fellowship with one another, and the blood of Jesus his Son cleanses us from all sin.'[10]

Or how about this encouragement from James Chapter 5,

> 'Therefore, confess your sins to one another and pray for one another, that you <u>may be healed</u>. The prayer of a righteous person has great power as it is working.'[11]

What are we seeing in these passages? As we meet with others in our community group, the confession of sin and bringing of our lives before others into the light is where healing takes place. Confession of sin to others in a community group sounds hard and horrible to most of us, but I guarantee you that when those within the group begin to experience the healing and life that comes as a result, and to see that people are in your struggles with you and have your back through the worst life can dish out, they will begin to see the benefit. Through the trials of marital problems, sin strongholds or whatever

10. 1 John 1:7
11. James 5:16

else the group members are facing, community like this can be a deep blessing. As sin is falling away and victory in Christ is found, everyone involved begins to see the benefit! As we read in Romans 13, 'But put on the Lord Jesus Christ, and make no provision for the flesh, to gratify its desires.'[12] One of the main ways we make no provision for the flesh is to let others know about our sin struggles.

The opposite of this Core Value is for a Christian to isolate him/herself and become a '*Lone Ranger*' Christian. I love the *Lone Ranger* as much as the next guy, but in this case, isolation does not lead to life! Proverbs 18 tells us that 'Whoever isolates himself seeks his own desire; he breaks out against all sound judgment.'[13] The wise Christian knows that he needs the protection, the accountability, and the prayer of others around him in order to prevail in all the areas God wants Him to. We will know that we are really living in the way God wants us to when we acknowledge our dependence, not only on God, His Word, and His Spirit, but also on each other.

Core Community Value #4: Exhort Continually toward Maturity

As you think of your disciple-making community group, it should be filled with people whom you consider to be friends: people who are speaking the truth to each other in love, who aren't afraid to lean into your life, ask questions of how things are going in your life and who are taking responsibility for one another. As we read in Colossians 3, 'Let the word of Christ dwell in you richly, *teaching and admonishing one another* in all wisdom, singing psalms and hymns and spiritual songs, with thankfulness in your hearts to God.'[14]

The word, admonishing in this context has a 'to warn' or 'to exhort' meaning, which fits much of what we read in Scripture about how these types of relationships should exist. 'Iron sharpens iron, and one man sharpens another.'[15] Developing a relationship with the others in a community group who are real friends, able to point out areas where you may be idle or need encouragement. is priceless. 'And we urge you, brothers, admonish the idle, encourage the fainthearted, help the weak, be patient with them all.'[16]

---

12. Romans 13:14
13. Prov. 18:1
14. Colossians 3:16
15. Prov. 27:17
16. 1 Thessalonians 5:14

I have found a key truth in this Core Value as I have developed these types of friendships. First, if they don't say something when they see areas of my life that need admonishment, I take that to mean that they don't believe me when I've told them I want to be the man of God that He wants me to be. I will often remind them that I want them to live out this role in my life because I so desperately need it.

Secondly, I've found that far too many people who call on the name of Christ choke out a major artery of Grace in our lives: those with whom we are in community are a means by which God expects us to sharpen and help and spur each other on. If you are going to be in God's community, this trait cannot be true of you.

Community Group Weekly Question #2

This question is generated to see how the person is doing in the areas of confession of sin, in repentance, knowing that 'If we say we have no sin, we deceive ourselves, and the truth is not in us.'[17] The question then to ask is, **'How have you fed your flesh?'** We each have something to confess each week... how are we leading each other toward repentance by sharpening one another through admonishing each other in a spirit of love, truth and grace.

Community Core Value #5: Give Biblical Counsel

As I wrote in the first book in this book series, a disciple of Jesus wants to be obedient to the Bible, and as we gather together within our communities in our churches, we need to emphasize in our small groups to be leading with biblical counsel. When we discuss issues that come up in each other's lives, it may be easier to lead with our own opinions and experiences as we offer advice and counsel. While opinions and experiences may have value, we must lead with the authority of Scripture.

As we read in 2 Timothy, 'All Scripture is breathed out by God and profitable for teaching, for reproof, for correction, and for training in righteousness.'[18] Because Scripture is inspired by God, this means that it has

17. 1 John 1:8
18. 2 Timothy 3:16

the authority to speak into each of our lives, and we should live every part of our lives subject to the authority of Scripture. The effectiveness of your community groups rises and falls on the biblical literacy of those in the group.

In relation to those within the community groups providing Biblical counsel, those within the groups may be wondering, 'How can I offer counsel from God's Word? I'm no professional!' The good news is that the group participants need only to be a student of God's Word. As we read in Romans 15, 'I myself am satisfied about you, my brothers, that you yourselves are full of goodness, filled with all knowledge and able to instruct one another.'[19]

Teach your community group leaders to always be asking, 'What does the Bible say about that?' It can become a fun exercise to search for answers during the meeting times or to give the group some homework to research and come to the next meeting with God's 'take' on the subject from His Word.

Finally, build an environment within your community groups to help each member and to then to put into practice the counsel from God's Word as it has been given, and to always be asking, "How can I make this truth from God's Word become reality in my life?" Those within the community group can help each person process and answer this.

If we don't apply God's Word to our lives and follow its teachings, we're just fooling ourselves.[20] Jesus said that those who hear His words and put them into practice are wise and have a solid foundation, but those who hear and don't respond are foolish people who will collapse when tough times come.[21] Each community group should make it their goal to encourage each participant to be personally in God's Word daily and lovingly bring God's Word before others.

Community Core Value #6: Great Commission Engagement

As I wrote about in some length in the first book in this series, I believe that the Great Commission—Jesus' command to proclaim the Gospel[22], make disciples[23] and be His witnesses in local areas and around the world[24]—is a command for all believers everywhere. Developing a culture within your community groups that life is a long-term missions

19. Romans 15:14
20. James 1:22
21. Matthew 7:24-27

22. Mark 16:15
23. Matthew 28:19-20
24. Acts 1:8

trip, with constant opportunities to proclaim Christ and each week gives us opportunities to impact people for Christ, is key for a healthy small group. As Paul so eloquently states in 2 Corinthians, 'we are ambassadors for Christ, God making his appeal through us.'[25] A community group can be the perfect place to encourage one another to be 'always be prepared to make a defense to anyone who asks you for a reason for the hope that is in you,'[26] by working together on how to share our testimonies and the Gospel. If there are some who do not know how to share their testimony or the Gospel, what a perfect place for the leader to shepherd the others in the class and lovingly teach them how to do this. One of the key things I've learned in interviewing disciple-making church leaders and through my research is that if there is no evangelism happening by the participants in a community group and no encouragement from one member of the group to another in this area, the group will largely become stagnant. Because of this, the leader of each group, together with the leaders 'up the line' in the levels above them should be regularly asking the leaders 'down the line,' together with those at their same levels, 'When was the last time was that you engaged with someone who is outside of a relationship with Christ?'

Community Group Weekly Question #3:

Because we don't want spiritual narcissists that are only thinking of themselves, we ask of each member, **'How have you fed others by way of evangelism and discipleship?'** This keeps the Great Commission commands on the forefront of peoples' minds, that they are a command for all Christians. As we explain this question to each person in each group, we also remind them that as Jesus gives us the commands of the Great Commission, he also then is challenging us, 'Why do you call me 'Lord, Lord,' and not do what I tell you?'

One final word about these three questions: Asking the questions to every member every week is a great way for you as an elder to show your church that you take the 'awake at 3am' verses seriously and that you really want people to be growing and thriving in their community groups. This is a key way that every member can be caring for every other member. On the

25. 2 Corinthians 5:20
26. 1 Peter 3:15

flip side, not asking the questions doesn't feel loving, as the heart behind the questions is not to be a spiritual hall monitor, but to be a loving heart.

Final Challenge to Elders and Pastors

I understand that doing community with this type of intentionality may be extremely difficult. In your responsibility in the 'awake at 3am' verses, I strongly believe it takes this intentionality to obey them well. Think of it this way: when my children were little, they would have wanted to eat jelly beans and donuts every day of their lives if I would have allowed them, but as their parent, I needed to ensure they were getting good nutritional food (with jelly beans and donuts only occasionally). Ask yourself the question, 'As one who is watching over the souls of my congregation, what do they *need* to be growing spiritually?'

Meeting in community in this way leads to life and peace. In Romans 8, Paul teaches about the difference between living in the flesh, which our flesh would love to do most of the time, or living in the Spirit. As he is making conclusions in his teaching, he writes, 'to set the mind on the flesh is death, but to set the mind on the Spirit is <u>life and peace</u>.'[27] Leading your people toward life and peace goes a long way in your pursuit to obey Hebrews 13:17 and Acts 20:28. Remember, as you get negative feedback from some of your people about the intentionality and frequency of the new community groups, that obedience—both yours to the Scripture passages you are responsible to obey, and their obedience as believers in Christ—is not determined by the outcome! If lot of people are grumbling, that is irrelevant to you because you want to be a 'God's Word says it, so we do it' kind of church.

---

27. Romans 8:6

Discussion Questions

1. After reading this chapter, do an assessment with your team on how you feel your church's current small group ministry is doing at helping your church become a disciple-making church. Use a separate sheet of paper to make a 'Going Well/Not Going Well' list of your current community groups.

2. What type of work is needed for you to develop a hierarchy for effective community group ministry as found in Exodus 18 that includes 'chiefs of thousands, of hundreds, of fifties, and of tens?'

3. Discuss initial thoughts about the 'Community Group Three Questions.' How could you best implement them into each of your current and future small groups at your church?

4. As an elder/church leader, how do you feel about fulfilling your responsibilities to the 'awake at 3am' verses? Better? Worse? About the same? Overwhelmed?

6

Fifth Mark of a Church that Makes Disciples

Commitment to Biblical Conflict Resolution

Christian leadership is a curious animal, especially in our churches. We must admit that it takes a lot of self-confidence to rise to the level of senior pastor or lead pastor of a church. The list of qualifications and qualities that are required to be a lead pastor or teaching pastor is lengthy. As I look at what it takes to fill this position, the list is quite daunting!

In addition to the qualifications of an elder described in Chapter 1, an extensive knowledge of Scripture sits toward the top of this list for most people. This range of knowledge doesn't come without a lot of hard work and study. I often think how hard it would be to be able to answer whatever question people might have about the Bible and be the one who could have most of those answers on the top of one's head! In addition to that knowledge, the ability to speak in front of groups and clearly communicate God's truths from Scripture is near the top of this list as well.

Although up to 75% of people in the United States report a personal fear of public speaking, also called Glossophobia[1], the senior pastor must be able to confidently stand in front of others and speak without fear. Many senior pastors are also expected to have certain administrative skills, especially

---

1. https://www.psycom.net/glossophobia-fear-of-public-speaking

when starting a church or leading a smaller church. Counseling experience and skills are nice to have too, since the pastor is often the one who is providing marriage or life counseling. And these skills are just at or near the top of the very long list of the duties a senior or lead pastor must be able to carry out. It is easy to see why some might think, 'I'm the Man around here…. this place couldn't run without me!' Because of this self-confidence, selfish ambition can begin to creep in and, far too often, this ambition kills servants of God and turns them into servants of themselves.

It's easy to see when this happens to senior leaders of churches. Their personal sense of worth goes up and down with how the church is doing in areas like attendance and giving. Terrified of failure, they know how to use people to get them where they want to go, and insecurity begins to creep in. In addition, ideas not personally developed by them are seen as a threat, because they weren't the ones to come up with the ideas. This ungodly ambition has taken out many talented lead pastors.

What makes Christian leadership an interesting study is that while it is good for our leaders to know that they are capable and qualified for the job, the Bible is full of advice for us that indicates that humble leadership actually wins the day. I could fill the rest of this chapter with passages on humility, but here are just a few:

- Paul's admonition in Romans 12, 'For by the grace given to me I say to everyone among you not to think of himself more highly than he ought to think, but to think with sober judgment, each according to the measure of faith that God has assigned.'[2]
- Jesus' brother James encourages us to, 'Humble yourselves before the Lord, and he will exalt you.'[3]
- Jesus gives us this admonition as he is telling the Parable of the Wedding Feast, 'For everyone who exalts himself will be humbled, and he who humbles himself will be exalted.'[4]

Secular sources also praise those who lead with humility. A recent *Wall Street Journal* article reported that researchers and employment experts increasingly have found that selecting humility as a key trait for company leadership yields better results than when that trait is missing: "Humility is a

---

2. Romans 12:3
3. James 4:10
4. Luke 14:11

core quality of leaders who inspire close teamwork, rapid learning and high performance in their teams, according to several studies in the past three years. Humble people tend to be aware of their own weaknesses, eager to improve themselves, appreciative of others' strengths and focused on goals beyond their own self-interest."[5] Researchers have found that humble leaders who are quick to both praise their employees and spread credit for a job well done see this practice as a linked with lower absenteeism and lower turnover. As we now look at the Fifth Mark of a Church that Makes Disciples--a church that has an ever-growing culture and commitment toward biblical conflict resolution--it is a Mark that begins and ends with top leadership being the first to lead with 'a limp,' leading with humility and being the first ones to seek out Biblical conflict resolution. When we see this mark in a church, we see a church who works hard at implementing biblical conflict resolution with vigor and rapt attention. When conflicts arise in this church, and specifically its leadership, does not shy away from leading those having the conflict from going through the processes and seeking a biblical conclusion to the conflict.

Conflict resolution is a Mark of a Church that makes disciples for a couple of key reasons. First, as we gather together as the body of Christ, the Lord wants us to maintain unity with one another. The apostle Paul makes this point clear in Ephesians 4 as he urged us to 'walk in a manner worthy of the calling to which you have been called, with all humility and gentleness, with patience, bearing with one another in love, eager to maintain the unity of the Spirit in the bond of peace. There is one body and one Spirit—just as you were called to the one hope that belongs to your call.'[6] Maintaining unity in the body of Christ is important, then, because it enables us to 'walk in a manner worthy of the calling' we've received as believers in Christ. Unity is one of the key ways the Holy Spirit works in our lives. The Holy Spirit enables us to have faith in Christ, bears the fruit of love in our lives and gives us a common trait of caring for one another. Our common convictions and care are from the Holy Spirit, prompting Paul to call it 'the unity of the Spirit.' As the secular world watches the church, they should observe us resolving conflict in a way that glorifies the Lord, edifies the body of Christ, and reflects the principles laid out in Scripture.

I admonish those of you who are elders and church leaders to make a

---

5. https://www.wsj.com/articles/the-best-bosses-are-humble-bosses-1539092123
6. Ephesians 4:1-3

big deal about this at your church. This is one of those values in the life of the church that matters deeply. As the neighbors all around us watch the churches that exist in our communities, knowing that most of our society does not want to dive into conflict and prefers to pretend that it does not exist, they should observe that the church is a place where conflict is managed and resolved well.

It Starts at the Top

Before we walk through the 'how to' of this Mark of a Church the Makes Disciples, let's talk about why I am including this matter of conflict resolution as a mark of a church that makes disciples. When done well at your church, both within your staff and your congregation, I believe that conflict will provide opportunities to glorify God, serve other people, and grow to be like Christ. For biblical conflict resolution to spread throughout your church DNA, I find repeatedly in my research, interviews and reading that it must begin eventually with your church staff, starting with the senior pastor. Think about the foundation you would build if your senior pastor would say to your staff, 'I don't care if you were only hired yesterday, if I said something in a meeting that was hurtful to you, I want you to come and see me so we can talk about it.' That leader's willingness to apologize and talk through the conflict, would begin to communicate to all that this Mark a core value of your church. The senior pastor might also say, 'Hey, if I frustrate you and I'm not hearing you well, you have my permission to call the elders with your concern, and you don't need to ask my permission if that time comes...I am giving you permission today.' When the staff learns to be regularly asking, 'Are we good with each other,' that action sets the example for the rest of the church congregation to follow.

You are probably familiar with Ken Sande, the founder and former president of Peacemaker Ministries and the original author of the '4 G's' of Peacemaking, which form the foundation for his Peacemaker's Pledge.[7] As we look at how to make a commitment toward biblical conflict resolution, Sande's '4 G's' are an excellent cornerstone that provide a framework upon which you can build a new DNA of biblical conflict resolution at your church. Let's set the stage for how you can resolve conflict in a God-honoring way.

---

7. https://www.cmalliance.org/resources/publications/peacemaking_principles_pamphlet.pdf

Let's assume that a conflict has occurred between two people in your church. This conflict may be between two staff members, a staff member and a member of the congregation, several members of the congregation between each other, etc. We must first remember that as people reconciled to God through the death and resurrection of Jesus Christ, we are called to respond to conflict in a way that is remarkably different from the way the world deals with conflict. You must enter this conflict believing that you may have opportunities to glorify God, serve other people, and grow to be like Christ. Therefore, in response to God's love for you and in reliance on His grace, you remember these principles as you sit down with the other parties involved and begin the process of finding reconciliation.

Glorify God First

As Christians, we want to glorify God in all that we say and do. Whether in our day-to-day lives, as we 'eat or drink, or whatever you do, do all to the glory of God,'[8] or in our work and ministry lives, we want to say to God, 'not to us, O LORD, not to us, but to your name give glory, for the sake of your steadfast love and your faithfulness!'[9] As Christians, we desire to acknowledge God's greatness and give Him honor because He alone deserves to be praised, honored and worshipped! As conflict arises, instead on focusing on our own desires or on what others may do, we can decide to rejoice in the Lord and bring Him praise as we depend on Him to give us everything we need to honor and glorify Him through the conflict. By God's grace, conflict can be used to glorify Him by trusting and imitating Him and as a reminder to 'get out of our own way' by thinking of the others involved and seeing this conflict resolution as a way to serve them, and for all parties involved to grow to be like Christ as we confess the sin we have brought into the situation and turn away from attitudes that promote conflict.

Go and Show Your Brother His Fault

In determining if a conflict rises to a level that needs to be addressed, I

---

8. 1 Corinthians 10:31
9. Psalms 115:1, one of my favorite passages to repeat to the Lord!

love the saying, 'Don't sweat the small stuff.' There may be a lot of conflict that you can choose to just overlook and move on, knowing that God's love covers a multitude of sins.[10] You know the kinds of conflicts I am talking about here. In our daily lives, we get to choose whether a situation we don't like will rise to the place of 'that wasn't okay.'

Here are some questions you can ask yourself when determining whether a disagreement has risen to the level of 'I need to go talk to them about that.' As you go through the questions, you can simply answer 'yes or no' to each question.

Was the offense seriously dishonoring to God?

Has it permanently damaged a relationship?

Is it seriously hurting other people?

Is it seriously hurting the offender himself?

My favorite indicator was one that I learned in my early days on staff with The Navigators. As I was being coached through a conflict situation, the coach said, 'A way to tell if a conflict can be overlooked is, if I go to bed and then wake up the next morning, and I realize that it's not bothering me anymore, I can overlook it. But if it's a matter or conversation that is still bothering me, then I really need to go address it.' By using these questions and counsel, you, your staff and your congregation will avoid a lot of meetings and will learn how to improve at overlooking minor offenses. Also, this counsel is great both for a conflict you might need to resolve, or if you must serve as a mediator between two people who can't seem to figure out how to find resolution between them. In either case the counsel is applicable, and by keeping to these principles, you are giving high priority to the process of biblical conflict resolution.

Get the Log out of Your Eye

It is so easy for us to want to look at our own situation first and to take care of ourselves first, but in our healthy and biblical conflict resolution efforts, we must be quick to see how we may have contributed to the conflict. We remember Jesus' admonition in Matthew 7 as he teaches us,

---

10. 1 Peter 4:8

'Why do you see the speck that is in your brother's eye, but do not notice the log that is in your own eye? Or how can you say to your brother, 'Let me take the speck out of your eye,' when there is the log in your own eye? You hypocrite, first take the log out of your own eye, and then you will see clearly to take the speck out of your brother's eye.'[11]

I've always been impressed by the speck vs. log terminology, because that's how it goes sometimes. We get so focused on what the other person is doing to contribute to the conflict, we forget that we have a much bigger concern to take care of first: the huge log sticking out of our own eye! This many times is the hardest part of this process because, admittedly, we find it hard to honestly look at how we have contributed toward the conflict in order to drive the process toward reconciliation. As we read in Proverbs 16, 'All the ways of a man are pure in his own eyes, but the Lord weighs the spirit.' [12] We definitely prefer to think 'our ways are pure,' but our perception of the situation may be off and incorrect, and many times we don't have all the facts of the situation at our disposal! Through this process, a third party may be needed just to help each side see the other side's perspective. Before going into the initial conversation, we must first ask the Lord for help with self-awareness regarding our part of the conflict.[13] This step is vital because when all those involved see that we are being quick to take responsibility for our own contribution to the conflict, it sets the atmosphere in the room in a positive direction. Be quick to admit fault when the Lord reveals it to you. This gives you a great opportunity to lead with that 'limp,' knowing you are not perfect and may have contributed toward the conflict. Sit down with those involved and hear each side of the story. [14]

Always try to listen for their feelings first, not the details of the issue at hand. It's an interesting phenomenon: if you do this, much of the time the issue resolves on its own! People often just want to be heard and feel understood, knowing that you truly heard how this conflict affected them and made them feel. As you address your side of the situation, always avoid using words like 'if,' 'but,' and 'maybe.' This tactic is often used by those who don't want to take responsibility for their actions. We don't want to be people who make excuses for our actions. Instead, we want to be quick to apologize[15] and

---

11. Matthew 7:3-5
12. Proverbs 16:2
13. 1 John 1:8
14. Matthew 5:23-24, Proverbs 6:1-5
15. Luke 15:21

ask the other party for forgiveness.[16] Be very direct and ask them, 'Will you forgive me for X?'

Often, people at this stage will say 'I need to tell you that I'm sorry for X.' Train yourself, your staff and your congregation to *directly ask* for forgiveness, rather than just admitting "sorry-ness." If any of your staff or congregation struggle with asking directly for forgiveness, help them and coach them until they get used to asking directly.

As forgiveness is given (hopefully!), begin the process of accepting the consequences[17] and altering your behavior.[18] If you follow this process and teach your congregation in conflict to do the same, you've done everything that you need to do as a believer.

An important point about asking for forgiveness: the other party may or may not forgive you, and you cannot control what they are going to do. Paul gives us guidance in this area as he writes, 'If possible, so far as it depends on you, live peaceably with all.' Our call is to live peaceably with all, and I think we've done that if we've earnestly followed these steps.

Gently Restore

Throughout this process, we want to be carefully considerate of the person or people involved and take Paul's advice to 'restore him in a spirit of gentleness.'[19] When an offense cannot be overlooked, we must approach them with a heart toward restoration, humility and love. We should want to help them learn and grow from the situation, recognizing that all sin is primarily against God.[20] We want them to grow and learn, just as we desire the same for ourselves. As we approach the other person, we must talk personally and graciously with those whose offenses seem too serious to overlook, seeking to restore them rather than condemn them. When a conflict with a Christian brother or sister cannot be resolved in private, we will then ask others in the body of Christ to help us settle the matter in a biblical manner.

16. Prov. 28:13
17. Luke 19:1-9
18. Ephesians 4:22-32, John 8:11
19. Galatians 6:1
20. Psalm 51:4

Go and be reconciled

At the end of this process, you want the relationship to be 'all good.' There should not be any resulting brewing or anger remaining on either side. If signs of 'brewing' continue you may need to go back through the whole process again and learn why.

At this stage, we should talk about true forgiveness. When someone else has taken responsibility for their actions, has done the good work of asking you directly for forgiveness, and tells you of a plan to change their behavior, genuine forgiveness needs to be given. This means that you choose to no longer dwell on what happened, nor should you bring it up to them and use it against them. ('Remember the time you did X?') After you've forgiven them, you must choose not to talk to others about the situation between you. ('Did you hear what Sally did to me?') Certainly, biblical forgiveness like we see in Colossians 3, where we are called as believers to forgive 'each other; as the Lord has forgiven you, so you also must forgive,'[21] should be generously given and the relationship with the other person should be restored. Remembering how much Jesus has forgiven you as you repeatedly trespass again Him and His commands goes a long way as you choose to forgive others of their trespasses against you.

Final Thoughts and Advice

Developing a church culture of being quick to resolve conflict helps you become a disciple-making church. There are a few final pieces of advice about this process that I've found useful and would like to share with you here.

First, as you develop this Mark into the DNA of your church, don't allow anyone to spread gossip in the form of talking about a potential conflict they had with someone else. Cut that conversation off quickly and be certain to say, 'I think you should go directly to that person and talk to them about this matter.' Allow this immediacy to be the new standard. The same counsel goes for someone who wants to tell you about a conflict they have, and then to ask you 'Please don't tell anyone else about this.' This is your cue to stop them right there, and develop a habit of saying something like, 'Since I am not a part of the problem or the

21. Colossians 3:13

solution, you probably shouldn't tell me that.' Perhaps the one exception here might be if they are coming to you with very limited information about the conflict, and their motive is to get counsel about how to handle it biblically. That situation is a little different, but in order to develop this DNA within your church, you'll want to help the parties involved learn to deal with each other directly.

As you make conflict resolution a high priority at your church and you begin to practice your commitment to biblical reconciliation, you must be prepared for unreasonable people! Sometimes, you may do everything right, follow all the steps and say all the right things, and it's still going to be a disaster. In this case, don't give up on your commitment to biblical reconciliation; just take a day or two to pray and wait for the Holy Spirit to work in their hearts, assess what went wrong, and then try again. In such instances, if the offense is serious enough, you may need to follow the Matthew 18 protocol that I assume you already understand:

> 'If your brother sins against you, go and tell him his fault, between you and him alone. If he listens to you, you have gained your brother. But if he does not listen, take one or two others along with you, that every charge may be established by the evidence of two or three witnesses. If he refuses to listen to them, tell it to the church. And if he refuses to listen even to the church, let him be to you as a Gentile and a tax collector.'

In situations like this, you will want to follow the steps closely, taking people with you as necessary. There may be a rare occasion where you must remember that you did everything to 'live peaceably' and 'forgive as Jesus has forgiven you' and you're going to have to leave the matter at that. In this case, from your perspective, you did everything you could, you've prayed through it, and you just have to give it to God.

As you can probably tell, I have a deep heart for this mark of a church that makes disciples. I've not seen it play out very well in the churches where I've been involved, but that doesn't mean it is not important; in fact, the unresolved conflict puts even more importance on this Mark for me. Because I have a deep heart to see Christians become fully devoted followers of Jesus, I know how effective this mark is at making disciples. In the Gospels, we see several occasions where Jesus implores us to 'deny ourselves.'[22] For those of us who want to follow Jesus, submitting ourselves to Him in all areas of our lives, 'denying ourselves' is part of that process. Denying ourselves simply means that we say 'No' to ourselves and 'Yes' to God. This is a daily substitution of what we want in our flesh in exchange for what God wants for our hearts and lives. Reinforcing biblical conflict resolution at your church forces people to set their own desires aside (I want to win this argument and show everyone that I'm right!) for God to be glorified, and the other parties and the relationship to be restored.

Discussion Questions

1. As you assess the DNA of your church, how has biblical conflict resolution entered that DNA and culture?

2. As a senior leader at your church, how well have you communicated that biblical conflict resolution starts with you, and that you want people to come to you to resolve any disagreement on their minds that involves you?

---

22. Mark 8:34, Luke 9:23

3. Have you gone through the '4 G's' with your staff and congregation? If so, how has that gone and what areas do you see you may need to refresh? If not, as you read this chapter, what thoughts come to mind about how you could get that started?

4. How effective are you and your church leaders at stopping potential gossip? How effectively do people resolve conflict without your involvement, when you are not a part of the problem or solution? If you've not addressed or taught this, can you see how it would help build biblical conflict resolution into your church's DNA?

7

The Sixth Mark of a Church that Makes Disciples

Membership as a Disciple-making tool

In my work at One Eight Catalyst, I occasionally get invitations to attend and participate in church missions conferences. I love attending them because I get the opportunity to talk about what we do with One Eight Catalyst, and to meet people who have a similar heart toward helping every Christian find Great Commission fulfillment. A couple of years ago, I was invited to a missions conference at a Baptist church in Spartanburg, South Carolina. At the missions conference, each missionary was assigned to a Sunday School class and, throughout the conference, that missionary gets to speak to their assigned class a couple of times—and usually, the group treats the missionary to a Sunday lunch at a local restaurant. One of the things I love most about my work is the travel, and in particular, getting to eat a 'local joints,' tasting the local food, whether in Spartanburg, Shanghai or Singapore.

When asked where I wanted to go for Sunday lunch, since I had never previously been to Spartanburg, I asked the class, 'Where is the most "local" place that you know of in Spartanburg—the restaurant that best represents the local food of this area?' After talking among themselves for a few minutes, one of the ladies said, 'I think we should take Mike to the Beacon Drive-In!' They proceeded to tell me a little of the history of The Beacon, and it did seem like it was the most 'local joint' in town. Started in 1946, the Beacon serves hamburgers, cheeseburgers and a whole host of Southern favorites including fried bologna sandwiches and fried okra. And at The Beacon, when you order your cheeseburger, the most local thing to say is, "I want a 'Cheeseburger-a-Plenty.'" The 'a-Plenty' part means that on the same plate as your burger, you will find a very generous helping of onion rings and French fries, so much so that you can't even see the burger under all the onion rings and French fries!

As the class chatted amongst themselves about The Beacon, some expressed a concern about going to eat there for our Sunday lunch. They worried that some people can't handle all the grease that goes into the food there, and some had previously had some bad experiences, including some very bad gastric problems. One lady approached me privately with somewhat dire words about how horrible her experiences had been there and how she just would never go back! At this point, I told the group that we didn't need to go there, knowing that there were probably some other local places that would do just fine, and in fact, please let's *not* go there if some would dread going there.

A very interesting thing happened then: everyone--including the lady who had spoken with dread in her voice, said 'No we definitely want to take you there!' At this point, I was thinking, 'Okay, so people want to take me there, but they dread going there? That makes a lot of sense!' Even my good friend Steve, who lives in Spartanburg and who had introduced me to this Baptist church, said when I asked him if I could treat him and his family to lunch at the Beacon when I came back the next year, 'Well, as a relative newcomer to the city, you should definitely go, but my father-in-law is ninety years old and I don't want to speed up his demise by taking him there!'

Mention the topic of church membership to many evangelical Christians and ask their thoughts on the topic, and many will offer a response like what Spartanburg locals say about the Beacon Drive-in. Yes, we need it--but no, I don't particularly like it!

When I asked some Christian friends of mine about their thoughts on church membership, I got a variety of responses:

> 'Yes, it's definitely important, but I don't particularly think it's necessary.'

> 'I understand we want to keep track of who's attending our church,

but it's seems like an outdated method designed to make sure people are tithing.'

'I know a case can be made for church membership, but I attended a church in my early 20's where church leaders used membership like a hammer to make us do what they wanted. It seemed like a method of control and I'm leery now of any church that has a membership process.'

It seems that if you ask ten Christians what they think of church membership, you get ten different answers! In this chapter, I want to show you that the Sixth Mark of a Church that Makes Disciples--which is a church that utilizes membership as a disciple-making tool--is the most important mark of the six and is the mark on my list into which every other mark feeds.

But before we get into all of that, I need to have a 'heart-to-heart' with the elders and church leaders reading this book. Throughout the course of this book, I have talked quite a bit about the passages of Scripture that I've called the 'awake at 3am' verses that elders should examine and use as biblical requirements for your work as overseers at your church. I'd like to add one more passage to this list of requirements for elders as they oversee the church for whom God has given them oversight.

I love the letters that Paul and Peter wrote to the churches that were planted in previous missionary journeys. As we read 1 Peter, we see Peter writing back to the churches that had been planted in modern-day Turkey, in an area where he may have had the opportunity to visit and preach. He sends them encouragement to stand strong in light of current persecution and writes words of encouragement to the elders. In Chapter Five, Peter writes to the elders of these churches,

'So I exhort the elders among you, as a fellow elder and a witness of the sufferings of Christ, as well as a partaker in the glory that is going to be revealed: shepherd the flock of God that is among you, exercising oversight, not under compulsion, but willingly, as God would have you; not for shameful gain, but eagerly; not domineering over those in your charge, but being examples to the flock.'[1]

I'd like to add this passage to our 'awake at 3am' passages, and really dig a bit into what your job is at your church and the responsibilities you have been given by God. You are charged with keeping watch over the souls of those in your congregation in a way that honors Jesus and will be required to give an account after your earthly life is over about how you did at keeping watch. In addition, you are charged to pay careful attention to all the flock– yes, the flock that the Holy Spirit gave you oversight of, and the flock that has been purchased by the very blood of Jesus! We now add to that the 1 Peter 5 requirements of shepherding the flock of God that is your church. Sheep need feeding and tending and guiding and protecting. You're called to do this with your people, exercising oversight in a way that doesn't bring you gain and is not domineering, but rather, is an example of godly living to your congregation. As you let all these responsibilities wash over you, I must ask you this: how much do these responsibilities concern you? Can you see biblically that when you accepted the invitation to become an elder, the responsibilities were so much bigger than just running a business meeting for your church from time to time?

As we look back at previous marks of a Church that Makes Disciples, we see the enormity of your responsibilities as an elder: Looking at these passages through your lens of a high view of Scripture and demonstrating that your 'doing' matches your 'saying' that the Bible truly is the inspired Word of God, you read these passages and a compulsion should come over you to want to obey them to the best of your ability. As you pray through your desire to see the Gospel transforming the lives of your people at your church, shepherding them, keeping watch over them, guiding them, and challenging them to be a fully devoted follower of Jesus are crucial activities. You need equipping tools and classes you've created in these responsibilities to equip them through training, and you're setting up a structure toward biblical community, both of which help them grow spiritually. As we wade into the deep waters of these responsibilities, may I offer you one more tool that finishes off these responsibilities and helps you do them to the best of your ability? Creating a membership process that follows Peter's instruction for you to shepherd the 'flock of God that is among you, exercising oversight--not under compulsion,

---

1. 1 Peter 5:1-3

but willingly–as God would have you; not for shameful gain, but eagerly; not domineering over those in your charge, but being examples to the flock.'

Clearly, Peter was hearing reports of elders who were domineering and used their position as an elder for 'shameful gain,' just like we see today in far too many of our churches. This membership process will help you achieve at least two key goals: first, it helps you as the elders in leadership know who you are responsible for shepherding and who you are giving an account for, and secondly, it will help your congregation know what you want to accomplish (remember my section on mission statements) and what they are signing up for. In Hebrews 13, they also have a part to play as they submit to your leadership, and we all know that it is really hard to ask people to submit to leadership if they don't share the vision of what the leader believes and stands for. As we start on the journey toward biblical membership, we begin by looking at two key passages that should guide any church at their core: the Great Commandment, and the Great Commission. We all want to love the Lord our God with all our hearts and with all our souls and with all our minds,[2] and as I stated in the Introduction, the Great Commission command to 'make disciples of all nations, baptizing them in the name of the Father and of the Son and of the Holy Spirit, teaching them to observe all that I have commanded you'[3] is a command that Jesus wants all His followers to obey. The obedience of these two passages plays out differently in different churches, but obedience is always the goal. For example, in a church located in the center of a major city, their vision may be to reach their city of 10 million people. For another church within a geographic area, they may focus on the call to all people to be fully devoted followers. In both cases, they are obeying the two commands, based on how God has guided and led their leaders to move forward. The final piece for the elders of either church is to determine how the revised 'awake at 3am' verses and passages are obeyed as they shepherd and care for the flock God has given them within the vision of ministry God has provided.

2. Matthew 22:36-40
3. Matthew 28:19-20

A Process for Elders toward Biblical Membership

I'd like to offer you a process toward biblical membership that you can follow for your church, enabling you as elders to know who you are responsible for shepherding and who you are giving an account for, and secondly, a process that helps your congregation know what you want to accomplish and what they are signing up for. While this process can be customizable to your church, sticking as close to the process I present here, according to my extensive research and interviews of elders who are doing this well, will help you accomplish the aforementioned goals that membership achieves.

It is a Process

The first point I want to stress here is that this is a process. As we see in the dictionary definition, the word *process* is defined as 'a series of actions or operations conducing to an end,'[4] a process that takes time and is a series of actions that lead toward a specific end. In this case, the 'end' is the people in your congregation becoming members of your church. Throughout this process, you will want to take your time because membership should be seen not as a privilege, but as a responsibility. People in your congregation who go through this process are agreeing to be corrected, to have people speak truth into their lives as a sign of the authenticity and accountability required for the evangelical Christian. On both sides, expectations need to be clearly laid out, so they there are no misunderstandings. The common view of membership is that it is just a formality to go through ("go to a class, sign a paper, and you're in") does nothing for you as an elder as you desire obey your responsibilities, and does nothing to help congregation members meet their requirements as well.

First Stage: Membership Classes

These classes are the 'first step' toward membership and give you the opportunity to share first at a '30,000-foot view,' covering topics like

---

4. https://www.merriam-webster.com/dictionary/process

why your church exists, what is the vision of your church, who you are as a church. These topics are intended to help people understand who they are considering joining, and to sense if it would be a good fit. I would recommend that you be very "up front" with those in attendance, explaining that these classes are intended for them to explore whether you church should be their church home.

For your part, work hard at honestly communicating that the goal of these classes is *not* to ensure that everyone who attends these classes becomes a member. Be okay with the idea that not everyone in the class will become a member. Go into the classes with the attitude that 'We're having this class as a way for you to find out if this church is the right fit for you.' Never take the attitude that 'we have one hundred people here, and we have failed if all one hundred people don't become members.' Start with the perspective that you are here to serve them, and to help them figure out if this church is the right place for them.

In subsequent weeks, you can begin to set the bar higher, communicating that you are able to call them to something much greater than themselves. As I have mentioned previously, I think it's good to set the bar high, knowing that while this may cause you to 'lose' some people, those who stay the course will be the type of people you want as members at your church. These people find excitement in being on mission with you in trying to accomplish something that no one can accomplish without God's involvement and intervention. You will want to explain the expectations clearly, so that no one is caught off guard later when the expectations are acted upon.

Doing a Relationship Check Up

At this stage, maybe as Membership classes are in their last session, you can ask each participant to submit a written testimony of how they received Jesus and believed in His name.[5] After reviewing these written testimonies, I highly recommend that you guide a team of volunteers whom you've trained to meet with each individual one-on-one to talk through his or her testimony in person. This can be a relatively simple conversation where two

---

5. John 1:12

commonly asked questions are asked:

- If you were to die tonight, on a scale of 1 to 10, 1 being the lowest certainty and 10 being the highest certainty, do you think you'd go to heaven?

- If you did die tonight, and you stood before God, what would you say when he asks you 'Why should I let you in?'

This one-on-one interview is a great way to ensure that those participating in the membership process really do know Jesus and are on the right track spiritually. In talking with several elders who are doing this plan, they reported the multiple ministry opportunities that these interviews provide to share the Gospel with those who actually do not know Jesus and have not surrendered their lives to Him. Many have come to know Christ in this way!

Develop a Membership Covenant

When your prospective members have been through your classes and the written testimony and interview process, I strongly believe that the next step in this process should be a covenant of some kind that has been designed for prospective members to sign.

Many churches fall short here, in my opinion. If you as an elder are doing your best to obey the 'awake at 3am' verses and you want to be clear that you as an elder are responsible for their souls, and to shepherd them well, this covenant is a great tool. Some will that say that this type of document is unnecessary, but the Apostle Paul reminds us that when we come into a relationship with Christ and we profess that He is our Lord and Savior, we are grafted into His body: 'For just as the body is one and has many members, and all the members of the body, though many, **are one body**, so it is with Christ. For in one Spirit we were all baptized into **one body**—Jews or Greeks, slaves or free—and all were made to drink of one Spirit.'[6] Since we are grafted together as one, let's describe clearly what that looks like. When you make expectations clear, you avoid becoming one of the many churches I've seen that are not executing on what the church

---

6. 1 Corinthians 12:12-13

is called to execute on, and you also avoid the hypocrisy, ineffectiveness and compromise we see when expectations for membership aren't clearly laid out. This document is the best way for each side to say, 'I agree with what you agree with, and coming together like this is important.'

As it relates to covenants, I often think of the covenantal relationship of the wedding vows. When I married my wife Sherie, I committed to certain things that went beyond just simple promises. I made covenantal promises to my wife to do my best at certain things, and I also made those promises to God. Standing before our friends and family, I made promises that, based on the Bible, 'glued' me together with my wife, as we read in Ephesians 5, 'Therefore a man shall leave his father and mother and hold fast to his wife, and the two shall become one flesh.'[7] To break these covenant promises is to break faith with God as well. A membership covenant is similar in that it gives you as an elder the opportunity to say, 'Here is what I am accountable for to you and to God, as I shepherd and keep watch over you, and here is what you as a new member of our congregation are committing to before me as your shepherd and before God.'

This Membership covenant is written in a manner that is consistent with the Word of God and clearly lays out what this new relationship looks like. For an example of a covenant that I think is very well written, find your way to the web site of my friends at Watermark Church in Dallas, and type in 'Covenant' to see how they tackled this document.

In addition to the Membership Covenant, I assume that you already have a doctrinal statement at your church, which simply is a 'Here's what we believe about the really important stuff' kind of document. This would include your church's belief statement about God, the Bible, the Holy Spirit, the Trinity, etc. I would recommend that at the same time that you ask people to sign the Membership Covenant, you ask them to sign another document which simply states that they agree with the doctrinal statement of the church as well. There should be agreement amongst your members that there are essentials of our faith upon which we all agree, and our signatures are evidence of our agreement with those essentials.

---

7. Ephesians 5:31

Join a Small Group

If you have implemented the small group ministry structure that I explained in Chapter 5, you have a perfect way to invite new members to begin plugging into a small group at your church. As explained in Chapter Five, your Exodus 18 hierarchy allows you to have a 'dotted line' from the elders all the way down to each individual person in each small group, allowing you to shepherd and give careful attention to your flock in your role as an overseer. If you truly believe that God has called you to shepherd your congregation and watch over their souls, urge each member to connect with others in a small group.

A couple of points to consider here: the churches that I have researched who have designed the process and small groups well usually only allow those who are members to be in these small groups. Their reason is that as the elders may need to step in as the church and address recalcitrant or repeated sin in a person's life, if that person is not a member, he or she may say something like "you don't have the authority to speak into my life in that area since I have not submitted myself to your leadership.' This does not allow you as an elder to keep watch or shepherd or oversee at all. Only with those who have agreed to enter into the Membership Covenant will you be able to say, "We see that you have signed the Covenant and our doctrinal statement, you have agreed to submit yourself to leadership, and you have added your signature signifying your commitment and agreement."

Select an Area (or two) of Service

Every church has plenty of opportunities for people to serve, and as new members join, getting them involved in both serving others and serving the Lord is a 'win-win.' For the fully-devoted follower of Christ, we recall the Apostle Paul's admonition that we are 'his workmanship, created in Christ Jesus for good works, which God prepared beforehand, that we should walk in them.'[8] In your Membership Covenant, you can carefully state that new members agree to serve others in ministry, and as people become new

8. Ephesians 2:10

members, providing a list of areas where they can serve in your church allows them to see ways they enjoy serving according to how they are gifted in their spiritual gifts.

I always recommend to new members, especially those who have not served much in a church, to try several different opportunities in an effort to find where they see God at work and to what areas they are clearly not called. For example, you would not want me to serve on a praise team or choir.... I can't sing to save my life! But I enjoy teaching Sunday School or leading a small group because that fits within my spiritual gift mix.

As people are serving, often remind them that 'Whatever you do, work heartily, as for the Lord and not for men, knowing that from the Lord you will receive the inheritance as your reward. You are serving the Lord Christ.'[9]

Develop an Annual Assessment

As you work heartily at obeying the 'awake at 3am' verses and passages, it would be a shame to put so much work into pressing in on how to best lead, guide and shepherd your congregation, only to not know how you are doing and what areas you are doing well and which areas you need to continue working to improve.

Several churches that I researched have developed assessment tools to help them assess their own successes and failures in these critical areas. This can be done in several ways, from an assessment that people complete online, to a workbook/paper version that is completed annually within the small groups. However you choose to have people participate in this assessment, I view it as an invaluable tool that will help you as an elder know how you and your church are doing in the areas where you've committed to excel. The questions you develop for the assessment are up to you and can be worded in any ways that will help you best assess your church's performance. These questions can run the gamut, but obviously it will be helpful to know how people feel about how they are doing spiritually, where they are serving in the church and their assessment of how their growth and participation is going for them, ways they are engaging at the church, and how they feel the church

9. Colossians 3:23-24

is doing at keeping them equipped for service, to areas of how they are doing outreach and how trained they feel to effectively share Christ with people they know or meet.

Many other types of questions can be helpful to you, and you can have a fun session or three talking with your elders and staff team about the types of things you'd like to know that would best help all of you to assess how you and your teams are doing. As the answers are returned to you, review and use them to assess your work as an elder and the areas that may need help as you attempt to do what you believe God is asking you to do.

Another main question as you develop an annual assessment is how you are going to get every member to fill it out every year. Finding what works best for you and your church is a fun challenge!

Final Thoughts: Ensure that Your Process Has Teeth

After working through this quite lengthy and thought-out process, the last thing you'd want to do is to have a process that has no "teeth" to it! Here are two examples of potential situations that could arise, as an explanation of what I'm talking about.

The first one is a situation that might occur during the membership process. Suppose that a young couple participate in the process of becoming members at your church, and you see on their forms that they have the same address, but they are not married. Although some would say 'We don't want to get into that, who are we to judge,' there are times that clearly a conversation becomes necessary. This is actually a great opportunity to sit down with the couple and talk it through with them. The loving thing to do would be to sit down and have a conversation which could go like this: 'At this point, John and Sally, we'd like to call you to faithfulness in this particular area of your lives, and as we walk with you toward that goal, let's set aside for now the goal of membership or to being in a small group.' Many times, these kinds of conversations go really well, especially if they are new believers, as it's possible that they didn't even know they were doing something wrong. I believe that these types of conversations, about any number of sin issues, are always an opportunity to love people, to share the Gospel, and to call them to a life of faithfulness. The second scenario is one that happened to a pastor friend of mine a couple of years ago. One of their church members, who had been struggling with homosexual feelings for years, had been meeting with the men in his small group who were loving him well and praying for him. For several years, he did well in resisting temptation and shared how, although he thought he had the 'unforgiveable sin,' he had found a community in this church who loved him well. As this temptation became 'too much' for him, he eventually told them that he no longer believed same-sex activity was inappropriate for a follower of Jesus, and he no longer desired to turn from it. After many conversations, both with this man and as an elder and staff team, my pastor friend and his elders, with great grief of heart, sent this man a letter informing him of a change in his membership status. As it was explained to me, the change in membership status was simply, 'Just like any member whose beliefs move away from the core commitments, biblical convictions, and values of our church (which were all laid out in the Membership Covenant), it became appropriate to formally acknowledge his desire to not pursue faithfulness to Christ with us. When you enter into a formal membership covenant with a church family, the leaders and church community promise to "keep watch over your souls," according to Hebrews 13:17, and will be held accountable before God for your spiritual care and encouragement. This care is a sacred trust and comes with great responsibility. As members of God's family we are called to love, admonish, encourage, and help each other in our relationship with Christ.'[10] With that statement, a letter was sent to this man, informing him both of their ongoing love for him, and that he was no longer a member of this church. In the letter, a path toward restoration was laid out, including tangible steps that could be achieved on this path.

We don't hear much anymore about church discipline, otherwise known as loving correction, because many churches seem to completely ignore it, even though the mandate is clearly laid out both by Jesus and throughout the New Testament.[11] As any parent knows, discipline is an act of love, and genuine correction is always meant to bring about good in the life of an individual. We see this in Hebrews 12, 'For the moment all discipline seems painful rather than pleasant, but later it yields the peaceful fruit of righteousness to those who have been trained by it.'[12] As you establish your membership process, you are wise to consider that these types of scenarios

---

10. https://www.watermark.org/statement
11. Matthew 18:1-5, 1 Corinthians 5:11
12. Hebrews 12:11

come up and you need to be ready for them. This is what makes membership a disciple-making tool: the elders are overseeing their congregation, the congregation has committed to this oversight, and all eyes are on Jesus as everyone walks and grows with Him together.

Discussion Questions

1. What does your church do in relation to membership? After reading this chapter, has your opinion changed on the need for a Membership process and what it should include?

2. With the addition of the 1 Peter 5 passage to the 'awake at 3am' verses, what focus do the elders have on their solemn responsibility as elders at your church?

3. Does your church already have a Membership Covenant? If not, are you compelled now to write one? Does the task seem daunting or doable?

4. Can you see how a proper membership process helps you fulfill the responsibilities you carry as an elder? After reading this chapter, what changes do you want to make to your church's current membership process?

8

Do You Believe in This Thing or Not?

    This book is the second in a series of books that we at One Eight Catalyst have created to accomplish our mission to help Christians find Great Commission fulfillment. The book series is called the *Six Marks* series because each of the books draws out the top Six Marks of each book's theme. When the idea was drawn up, I was very enthusiastic and signed on to write the first couple books in the series. But when the time came to begin sketching out what the top Six Marks of a church that made disciples were, I quickly realized that I had a problem! The book series already had its title, but in my outlining, I found that we had seven key Marks of a Church that Makes Disciples! Through a process of elimination, I found that five of the Marks were so important that I couldn't leave one out, and that left me with the remaining two Marks and a decision. After some prayer and discussion, I decided that a Commitment to Biblical Conflict was also key, so that gave us Six Marks of a Church that Makes Disciples. Without giving it its own chapter, I wanted to at least give an honorable mention the Seventh Mark of a Church that Makes Disciples: a church that helps its congregation members make every day a missions opportunity.

Making Every Day a Missions Opportunity

In many of our Western churches today, I find that the Great Commission—the command Jesus gives to all Christians to proclaim the Gospel, make disciples, and be His witnesses in our local area and around the world—is a concept viewed by many Christians as an activity that is "only for the missionaries." And yet, in my reading of the New Testament, it seems clear that missional engagement is a command for *all* Christians, as Jesus gives us both the commands themselves, plus indications that obedience to those commands is a way to demonstrate our love for Him.[1]

One of the errors in thinking that many church leaders continue to propel forward is that missions happens only when we 'go on a missions trip.' As you continue to work hard at becoming a disciple-making church, I encourage you to also work very hard at breaking down this misconception, and instead promote the concept to your church that, wherever your people are, whether at home, at work, with family, or somewhere overseas, they are *on mission* at all times, not just when they go on a mission-focused trip. It seems clear to me through Scripture that wherever God has positioned us at a particular time, we have the opportunity to be an extension of His Church, to be 'salt and light' wherever we are. In the Sermon on the Mount, Jesus extols us to 'let your light shine before others, so that they may see your good works and give glory to your Father who is in heaven.'[2] Every day for the Christian becomes a missions opportunity, not just when we get on a plane and travel overseas.

In order to promote the concept that all of your congregation members are on mission for Jesus every day, let's picture four rings of influence for the Gospel that we all have as Christians. The first ring represents the neighborhood where we live. When I talk about this with people, I love to take out a sheet of paper and ask them to draw out their neighborhood with their house and the seven closest houses to their own. Then I ask, "Would you tell me the names of the families that live in each of these houses, and tell me one or two key concerns or challenges they face that you could be praying about on their behalf?" I am surprised by how few names most people know of those whom they live so near to every day. These families in our neighborhoods

---

1. John 14:15, Luke 6:46
2. Matthew 5:13-16

comprise our 'Jerusalem,' and as you oversee your congregation, help them begin to understand that the first ring of influence they can have in obeying the Great Commission is to get to know their neighbors, learn their story, and find a few ways to regularly pray for them. Invite your church to read through *The Art of Neighboring* [3] by Jay Pathak and Dave Runyon with you and talk with them about the authors' ideas for helping Christians think through strategically how to neighbor well.

In Chapter Seven, I mentioned the idea of creating an annual assessment, and one of the assessment questions could be, 'What is working for you as you are missionally engaging with people in your neighborhood?' The answers will give you real-time data on what is working, and you could post the ideas on a page on the church website for others to use. You will find creative ideas coming through as you emphasize the awesome opportunities, we all have to engage with our neighbors!

The Second Ring of Influence would be our workplaces. Seek out ways to encourage your congregation to think about their vocation as missions and try to find ways to see how people can use their vocations as a tool for becoming 'salt and light.' One of the best ideas I have heard was how a church had created 'vocational affinity groups,' where lawyers, architects, engineers, health care providers, teachers, and others came together with others in their fields to discuss together how they could use their professional expertise toward missional engagement. As the vocational groups meet regularly, they are encouraging each other, reading books and processing together an answer to the question, 'How can we use this skill set we are already passionate about to love and serve our city?' Starting to organize groups like this at your church would be a great way to see God at work within shared vocational interests to promote connection, equipping toward engagement and then deployment as they reach their city together.

The Third Ring of Influence for your congregation would be the city where you live. The 'impact areas' of focus that you as an elder board select can run the gamut from poverty alleviation to prison ministry, health and wellness, etc. Asking a volunteer to oversee each of these areas gives new and old members alike places to plug in and serve their city. These areas of focus are also a great way for community groups to plug in and serve together. As you develop your Exodus 18 'chiefs of thousands, hundreds, fifties, and tens'

3. Pathak, Jay and Dave Runyon, The Art of Neighboring. Baker Books, 2012.

model, those who oversee groups of Communities can teach and train the Community Group leaders about the theology of service, and if serving is a requirement for membership at your church, this is a good way for that requirement to be 'actualized.'

We have now reached the final ring, which is 'to the ends of the earth.' As some of the people in your church focus on reaching neighbors and those in their workplace, they may begin to ask about how they may participate in taking the Gospel overseas as well. While you will hopefully have some who will go to serve overseas, please also allow me to put a 'bug in your ear' for developing ways to reach those currently living in your community who have come from other countries.

If there is a university nearby, you will have an opportunity to include international student ministry. Many of these students are or will be future leaders back in their home countries, and you may have the opportunity to reach them for Christ while they are in your area. A friend shared this statistic recently: 40% of the people now moving into Dallas County in Texas are foreign-born! Here in Denver, Colorado, Denver Public Schools has counted 145 languages spoken by their students' families.[4] Probably some people live all around you that you could invite to your home, showing hospitality, which would lead to opportunities to share Jesus with them through the new and emerging friendship.

I offer one final note on encouraging your congregation to make every day a missions opportunity: I've heard it said that mediocre leaders think in terms of programs, and great leaders think in terms of values. Far too many churches think of outreach as a program, when it really should be a high value of people seeking missional engagement in their daily lives. This concept gets a special emphasis in this chapter, because as you build this value into the fabric of your church, it will be the result of many of the other Marks of a Church that Makes Disciples in this book. If missions is truly an embedded value at your church, it begins with the membership process and emphasizing it in your covenant, and then works its way through to your community groups and into your equipping classes. Much of the work you put into these other marks shows itself as your members, growing as disciples of Jesus, begin to seek opportunities toward missional engagement. Fully devoted followers of Jesus

---

4. https://www.denvergov.org/content/dam/denvergov/Portals/643/documents/Offices/Office%20 of%20Immigrant%20and%20Refugee%20Affairs/ImmRef_Assessment.pdf

just can't help but to share what He's doing in their lives, and they will want opportunities to be 'salt and light.' You can fan the flames, taking missions from a 'program' to becoming a church-embedding value, by preparing your annual message on Matthew 28 and Acts 1:8 and intentionally adding, "This is something we all do here!"

Do You Believe in this Thing, or Not?

One of my favorite sports movies of all time is the 2011 movie *Moneyball*,[5] starring Brad Pitt. It tells the story of Major League Baseball's Oakland A's and their 'miracle' 2002 season. and how they tied the American League record of twenty consecutive wins. What makes the story interesting to me is the process that Billy Beane, the general manager of the A's, uses to put together the 2002 Oakland A's. He was the first general manager in the Major Leagues to put into mainline use a process best known as *Sabermetrics*, an evidence-based analysis of baseball players and their statistics. This process that allowed Beane to replace high performing players who signed with other teams with players that were undervalued but had good statistics in key areas. Instead of looking at players based on their talent and future potential, he chose players based on how often they get on base. And in baseball, the more that players get on base, they greater potential a team has to score runs! So, with Sabermetrics, you're simply buying runs when you pay particular players with higher "On Base Percentages" over other players with a lower percentage.

One of my favorite scenes in the movie is when General Manager Billy Beane, frustrated by another season where the A's make the playoffs during the 2001 Major League Baseball season, only to lose in the first round of the playoffs, has his first meeting of the offseason with his top baseball scouts. As the scene opens, we see seven older men—presumably all scouts—talking about which prospects they like for the upcoming season to replace three key players that the A's lost to free agency. Billy sits at the 'head' of the table, listening to the men discuss the players they like best. As the scouts are talking about certain players, they are using terms like, "nice jaw," "this guy's got a little 'hair on his ass,'" "clean cut, good face" and when talking about the negatives of one player, one of the scouts says, 'he's got an ugly girlfriend.' When another

---

5. *Moneyball*. Directed by Bennett Miller, Columbia Pictures, 2011. Film.

scout questions that assertion, the same scout says, "'Ugly girlfriend' means he has no confidence." These scouts were doing things in the same way that scouts have done them for 150 years, but Billy Beane was sold on seeing how Sabermetrics would work in his baseball club, especially given the relatively low payroll he had to work with, given that the A's are a 'small market' team. Billy wasn't interested in the old ways that these scouts were using to replace the players that had left the A's; he was only interested in what percentage of the time players got on base—which upset the scouts as they continued to do things in the 'old way.'

I see an analogy between this baseball story and what is happening in many western churches. The assumption in today's modern church is that there is a *one size fits all* formula for seeing growth in your church, a formula that has worked forever. I recently did a Google search on 'formula for Church growth,' and a number of web sites that popped up in the search offered actual 'formulas' to see growth in your church! Add a second service, welcome church visitors well, invest in the next generation, get your church online, attract a crowd through large events, and on the list goes. Of course, as a church leader, you may want to do all of that, but it seems clear to me that you would want to focus first on a Sabermetrics for church growth: two key areas that you as a church leader or elder should have as your focus.

First, do everything in your power to ensure that everyone at your church and every decision you make leads your congregation toward growing better at being disciples of Jesus and making disciples of the people in your congregation. And if I haven't made it clear enough, the second Sabermetric for church growth is for the elders at your church to take extremely seriously the three 'awake at 3am' passages and determine how serious they want to be about obeying them. These two areas are the 'beginning and end' of becoming a church that makes disciples. Hopefully as you've gone through this book, you've grown determined to do both of these areas exceptionally well.

As you've seen throughout the course of this book, doing these two areas with excellence is incredibly hard. In my research and interviews, I've found that the elders and senior/lead pastors in particular must become almost obsessive about these two areas, because the winds that lead to drifting away from them in the church is a strong and persistent gale. The Enemy would certainly want you to fail at being a church where people are growing spiritually,[6] where sin is regularly confessed, unity within the body is growing by leaps and bounds as Biblical conflict resolution becomes normative, and the teaching and training of believers grows and leads to more confidence in Christians who are proclaiming truth in their neighborhoods, workplaces and around the world.

I offer three key steps for you to make progress on being able to do these two things with excellence.

1. Make the goal clear.

In Chapter 1, I encouraged you to have a God-given, clearly articulated and widely accepted reason why your church exists; that is, a clear mission statement for your church. All too often, the churches who don't have this clear directive cannot lead people to a place that isn't widely identified and known. Knowing why God organized your local church into existence—based principally on a biblical foundation—together with the responsibilities that God gives to elders in the 'awake at 3am' verses, is the first step becoming a Church that Makes Disciples. A clearly articulated mission goes a long way, especially if the leaders are saying it repeatedly and taking action[7] toward accomplishing it. Many churches have a mission statement that is never discussed and is apparently locked in a drawer somewhere so that leaders can pull it out when it's asked about–but why would you do that?

2. How clearly did God speak to you about your mission?

Let's assume that as you have gone through the process of writing a mission statement (Chapter 1), it has gone through the vetting process, and you have landed on a mission statement on which both the elders or pastoral staff and key lay leaders agree. After you have read through this book and set about the steps and processes in order to fulfill the mission you believe God has given you to accomplish through your church, I guarantee you that there will be pushback! Depending on how closely you have already been doing the mission that you're now determined to do, the pushback may be significant.

I believe that the main reason more elder boards aren't 'all in' on their churches' being great at becoming and making disciples is because they don't want to have to deal with pushback from others. They know that people like

---

6. John 10:10
7. James 1:22

and enjoy their church just the way it is, and why should they mess up a good thing? After all, people come to church services, they tithe, the elders can keep the lights on, staff are paid on time and they don't ask much of the congregation because, again, people like the way things are now. The principles in the Six Marks I write about have been around for a long time, as we read in Ecclesiastes, 'there is nothing new under the sun.'[8] As a pastor friend of mine said about the first book in this series, "Mike, you have brought out the ancient truths in a fresh, new way."

In the movie *Moneyball*, there's another scene I really like. Billy Beane gets an offer to become the General Manager of the Boston Red Sox after the initial success of the A's under the new Sabermetrics model of selecting players, which is a higher profile job than the one he's had with the A's. More money would be available for players and his salary would increase a lot too. Later in the movie, it's made known that with this new job, he'd become the highest paid General Manager in all of sports. If you haven't seen the movie, let me replay the monologue the actor portraying the owner of the Red Sox says to Billy during his visit to Boston.

> 'I know you're taking it in the teeth out there (since Billy was the first one to use Sabermetrics and succeeded at it), but the first guy through the wall, he always gets bloody. Always. This is threatening not just a way of doing business, but in their minds, it's threatening the game. (In your case, it's threatening church as those pushing back have known it) Really, what it's threatening is their livelihood, it's threatening their jobs. (Which actually could happen at your church if staff members aren't willing to get on board) It's threatening the way that they do things. And every time that happens, whether it's a government, a way of doing business, whatever, the people who are holding the reins, they have their hands on the switch, they go bats**t crazy. I mean, anybody who's not tearing their team down right now and rebuilding it using your model, they're dinosaurs. They'll be sitting on their ass on the sofa in October watching the Boston Red Sox win the World Series.'[9]

Recently I talked with a friend who serves on the pastoral staff of a church, and he lamented to me about how his church of 275 could not

---

8. Ecclesiastes 1:9
9. *Moneyball.* Directed by Bennett Miller and Produced by Columbia Pictures, 2011.

compete with the larger churches in his area in the areas of programs and services they could provide. Please, Pastor or Elder reading this right now, listen carefully as I tell you what I told him. Don't worry about providing every program under the sun until you have become great at the mission that God has given you to do. Allow me to repeat what I wrote in the Introduction regarding my colleague Todd Wagner's counsel about those in many congregations: 'Whether consciously or otherwise, they ask themselves questions that reveal their expectations. *Do I like the music in the ballroom? Do I like the captain and his staff? Do I get good service? Is it pleasant and comfortable? Do I like the experience enough to sail with them again?*'[10]

Please let me encourage you to become almost maniacal (in a good way!) about doing the thing that God has given you to do, because that's where a lot of church leaders make a mistake. If you have a church that is growing in becoming a disciple of Jesus, you'll find organic church growth for the reasons I've detailed in this book. At that point, you can begin to add various programs that may help you meet your mission. And when I say you have to be almost maniacal (characterized by ungovernable excitement or frenzy[11]) about the Six Marks I've outlined in this book, that means you are on an unrelenting pursuit in doing your straight best at accomplishing them.

What does this look like? As you set the course to be a church that is excelling in the Six Marks detailed in this book, distractions will happen. You must re-set the course continually so as to stay on course. Every new opportunity that comes across your desk must now go through a filter that asks the question, "Does this opportunity empower us or distract us from accomplishing the Six Marks, and the mission that God has given us?" To some at your church this determination might be viewed as 'mental' or 'psycho!' But if you'll stay the course, I can guarantee that you'll be glad that you remained hypervigilant.

3. Track Your Performance.

Determining ways to track how you are progressing at accomplishing the mission that God has given you is important. I recently read an article from the website boardview.io, which stated that '80% of small business

10. Wagner, Todd. Come and See: Everything You Ever Wanted in the One Place You Would Never Look. Colorado Springs, David C Cook, 2017. p. 79
11. https://www.merriam-webster.com/dictionary/maniacal

owners don't keep track of business goals,'[12] so goals are being set, but the progress toward those goals is not being measured. As a leader in a church, ensuring that your maniacal focus on the Six Marks in this book and the mission God has given you are being accomplished is important. I have found that two markers—tracked in the form of two questions—should be used to track performance of your church:

The first question is, "Are more people in your congregation catching on to the vision path where you are leading them?" The second question: "Are you accomplishing the goal to have more people become fully devoted followers of Jesus?"

Notice that I didn't mention increased attendance as a marker for success. While God may certainly lead more people to your congregation, the biblical markers seem to be aligned much more in obedience to the 'awake at 3am' verses for elders and the biblical command to 'go and make disciples.' Don't get caught in the trap that states that church attendance is the best marker toward church health. Many churches may have three hundred people or less on a Sunday morning, but they are doing a great job of being and making disciples! Be faithful with the people God has given you!

Final Encouragement

As I begin to round third base toward home plate, I'd like to give you, the reader, some final encouragement. I hope that by now you know how important I think the 'awake at 3am' passages are and how seriously I hope you are meditating on them. As I review some of the key imperatives from these passages, I continue to be deeply struck by their message:

- Pay *careful* attention to *all* the flock....
- Care for the church of God, which he obtained with *his own blood*....
- Shepherd the flock of God that is among you, *exercising oversight*, not under compulsion, but willingly, as God would have you....
- Not for shameful gain, but eagerly; not *domineering* over those in your charge, but *being examples to the flock*...
- (The elders are) keeping watch over your souls, as those who will have

---

12. https://boardview.io/blog/goal-setting-22-mind-blowing-stats/

to *give an account....*

Being a Christian church elder is not an exercise in weakness nor of inaction. It is certainly not something to get into if you have a hard time taking the lead and standing up for biblical truth. And it's most certainly not a good choice for someone who wants to do it because of the status it might portray to others in the church. You must be willing to serve because you want to fully obey what God has called you to do in this position and the way that God has put you right in the middle of people's lives, to help them grow spiritually and become fully devoted followers of Jesus. God wants us all to become disciples of Jesus, and you as an elder have an incredible opportunity to see God working through your words, your example, and through the position of influence that you have in the lives of your congregation. Do your best to pour everything you have and everything Scripture gives you into the lives of the people you influence.

We know that living as a fully devoted disciple of Jesus is hard, and it is costly, and to live with radical abandonment for His glory will definitely cost us something. Jesus tells us, "If anyone comes to me and does not hate his own father and mother and wife and children and brothers and sisters, yes, and even his own life, he cannot be my disciple. Whoever does not bear his own cross and come after me cannot be my disciple.'[13] And we're likely all familiar with the verses that come immediately after the 'abide in me' passages of John 15, "Remember the word that I said to you: 'A servant is not greater than his master.' If they persecuted me, they will also persecute you."[14]

Your congregation needs your best. They need you to pour everything you have into finding success in building the *Six Marks of a Church that Makes Disciples* into your church. Why? Because the members of your congregation will find it so much harder for your congregation to know how to give their very lives for Christ if they do not see it modeled in your life, if they have to wonder if it's all that important to you.

This work requires your best efforts because, while it is true that the cost of following Jesus and of being a biblical elder is high, I submit to you that the cost of *not* leading your people to be fully devoted followers of Jesus in the ways I've described in this book is infinitely higher. I weep over the thought of scores of churches, each under a banner of Christianity, that are

---

13. Luke 14:26-27
14. John 15:20

soft and have never counted the cost to follow Christ. Far too many elders and pastors have made deals with their people that implies, "If you'll give us enough money to keep the lights on and continue with fun programs, we won't ask much of you—and together we'll say we are all doing everything God wants us to do." There is a great cost to be paid for all who settle for this casual connection with Jesus, and they are missing out on the abundance, joy and satisfaction that He has designed for us.

Great Commission fulfillment requires fully devoted followers at its core, and the cost of nominal Christianity will be great also for those around the world who have never once heard the name of Jesus. Here is an example: according to my good friends at Joshua Project, over two billion people on earth have never once heard the name of Jesus, and 81% of all Hindus, Buddhists and Muslims do not personally know a Christian.[15] Christians in our congregations who are not fully devoted followers are content to allow these statistics to stand, whereas fully devoted disciples of Jesus want to tell others about what He has done in their lives. And at One Eight Catalyst[16], we exist to solve this inequity: on one hand, you have a Western Church that is more than financially equipped to reach all those who are yet to be reached, but 42% of the world's population remains unreached by or unengaged with the Gospel of Jesus. We need more fully-devoted followers, equipped and ready to go to the most remote places to reach those who do not know Christ!

And so, it comes down to this: as you meditate on the 'awake at 3am' verses, review the biblical purpose of the church outlined in the Introduction of this book, and look at both the biblical commands Jesus gives to all Christians--including those in your church, and remember the oversight you're called to provide, and remember the call in Ephesians for you to 'equip the saints,' I ask you the same kind of question that Billy Beane asked Peter Brand[17] "Do you believe in this thing or not? Do you believe that God has called you to do your absolute best at all of this—that what you state you believe plus what you are actually doing in your church does equal what you actually believe? And that the people in your congregation are getting all kinds of clues from you about what 'bearing your own cross and coming after Jesus' looks like?"

When rigorously applied in your church, the Six Marks of a Church

15. https://joshuaproject.net/resources/articles/has_everyone_heard
16. OneEightCatalyst.org
17. Peter Brand represents the real-life Paul DePodesta and is the actual 'architect' of how Sabermetrics was first applied within the A's organization. https://www.wsj.com/articles/SB10001424053111903927204576573271216641158

that Makes Disciples may be a major overhaul for your church. You as the senior pastor or elder must be sold out to applying them at your church, and you will need to ask yourself, each other and those on your staff habitually, "Do you believe in this thing or not?" You will have to believe that seeing the application of these six Marks will help you obey what God is calling you to do as an elder, and that a church full of growing, fully-devoted followers of Jesus is infinitely better than *not* obeying what God has called you to do as an elder and *not* having a church full of growing, fully-devoted followers of Jesus.

Do you believe that to be true today?

In the movie *Moneyball*, a decision needs to be made regarding whether to trade first baseman Carlos Pena, who manager Art Howe prefers over Scott Hatteberg (who has a much higher on-base percentage and who Billy Beane prefers). By trading Pena, Art Howe would be forced to play Hatteberg. When the decision is made to trade Pena, Billy's response to Peter's worry is such a fitting way to end this book.

Billy (to Peter): *It's a problem* that you think we need to explain ourselves. Don't, to anyone, ever. Now I'm going to see this thing through, for better or worse. Are we going to win more games with Pena or Hatteberg at first (base)?

Peter: It's close, but theoretically, Hatteberg.

Billy: What are we talkin' about, then?[18]

Elder or Lead Pastor, God has given you a tremendous responsibility in your role at your church. *It's a problem* if you think you need to 'dumb down' the church experience for those in your congregation. It's a problem if you want to 'take it easy' on them for fear of people leaving or not liking you as much.

Go the full distance in what God has called you do. Don't just preach about the need for the people in your congregation to reach their neighbors! Teach them how to do it!

Don't just set up Community Groups because you think you need to be doing it. Set them up so that those in your small groups can experience true life change.

---

18. *Moneyball,* 2011.

Become manic about those on your staff and in your congregation becoming great at biblical conflict resolution.

It's a problem to do anything less than your absolute best in all these areas. In a passage you probably repeat often, we get our motivation to do our best through the apostle Paul's great words, 'Whatever you do, work heartily, as for the Lord and not for men, knowing that from the Lord you will receive the inheritance as your reward. You are serving the Lord Christ.' While on earth, work hard to do your best, knowing that in heaven, there is both an inheritance and a speech waiting for you.

Discussion Questions

1. At your current church, is Missional Outreach more of a program or a value? If it's just something some people do some of the time, can you see the value of making it an integral part of what everyone in your congregation does all the time?

2. In this chapter, I am encouraging you to do two things really well, to the point of them being an obsession: Making every decision you make leads your congregation toward being better at being disciples of Jesus and making disciples of the people in your congregation and for you as an elder at your church to take extremely seriously the three 'awake at 3am' passages and determine how serious they want to be to obey them. How well do you think you as an elder/church leader are doing at these two things? What could you do better in these two areas?

3. As a way for you to process through the 'awake at 3am' passages, use this space to jot down thoughts that could be later shared with your fellow elders and church leaders about what it would take for you do each of these with excellence:

> Pay **careful** attention to <u>all</u> the flock....

> Care for the church of God, which he obtained with **his own blood**....

> Shepherd the flock of God that is among you, **exercising oversight,** not under compulsion, but willingly, as God would have you....

> Not for shameful gain, but eagerly; **not domineering** over those in your charge, but **being examples to the flock**...

> [The elders] are keeping watch over your souls, as those who will have to **give an account**....

4. What thoughts come to mind when you read my challenge in this chapter: Do you believe in this thing or not?' Do you think you believe in helping each of your people in your congregation to be a fully devoted disciple of Jesus?

If you don't, why not?

If you don't, is it time for a new career?

Additional Notes:

www.ingramcontent.com/pod-product-compliance
Lightning Source LLC
Chambersburg PA
CBHW081255040426
42452CB00014B/2514